820.9
Wolfe, Humbert
    Dialogues & monologues

WITHDRAWN

Date Due

OCT 07

Dialogues & Monologues

Dialogues & Monologues

HUMBERT WOLFE

Essay Index Reprint Series

BOOKS FOR LIBRARIES PRESS
FREEPORT, NEW YORK

First Published 1929
Reprinted 1970

INTERNATIONAL STANDARD BOOK NUMBER:
0-8369-1818-5

LIBRARY OF CONGRESS CATALOG CARD NUMBER:
74-121515

PRINTED IN THE UNITED STATES OF AMERICA

Contents

GEORGE MOORE

George Moore

121 EBURY STREET is not in itself a distinguished house. I do not know the architectural date of the street. I hazard the guess that, except for the Queen Anne houses of the Sloane Square end, it was washed up by a tidal wave from Belgravia, and left high and dry by the ebb. It has been decaying slowly ever since, as is the habit of jetsam abandoned by the sea.

It is a street chiefly of lodging-houses. Its population is essentially migratory, few being hardy enough to endure immolation for long in its deserted sea-caverns. It is much frequented by reasonably affluent youth on its arrival in Town; its quiet tends, therefore, to be marred during the night-season by a stir of cabs, and occasionally by cheerful outcries. But for the most part of the day the street is sullenly drowsy, land-locked, and lost in the marshes.

George Moore chose this street for his dwelling-place many years ago, though it taxes the mind to discover both why he went and why he stays. He has an explanation of both facts, but the explanation need not be taken too seriously. It is difficult, of course, not to believe it when it is advanced in the most persuasive voice of his time. A curious voice that owes its effect, not to the Irish intonation (so irritatingly attractive to the sentimental English), but to the queer contrast between the hard bones and the soft flesh that covers them. It is like one of those *soufflés* with ice in the heart of them. It cajoles and strikes.

But it is not only of the voice that you must beware. His conversation has the apparently indolent finish of his written style. There is no strain, no ambition in it. He speaks amiably and easily, for example, of some great contemporary reputation. Nothing, you are led to suppose, could be more artless, less prepared. But, when you reflect upon it afterwards, you will realise that you have, in fact, witnessed a performance. The room, for example, has no airs, and yet there are those three or four startlingly good pictures unobtrusively assaulting the mind from the wall. The tea which he offered was surely ordinary, and yet where else ever was that effect of a reception produced merely by the appearance of a tea-pot. Then there is George Moore himself, with a face carefully designed to disarm suspicion. The New English Art Club used to paint him to that extent that Max once drew a picture of a revolt of Chelsea models on hearing of Mr. Moore's return to London. But none of them ever disclosed his secret. He looks from their canvases, as he does in life, through ingenuous, wide eyes. He retains the curves of youth, and, if you are not careful, you will catch yourself wondering why he doesn't brush the white dust out of

his hair. Above all, his hands are disgracefully innocent.

These things, you observe, were his accessories.
The scene was set as a background to the apparent care-
lessness of his sentences. When you record them in
your mind, you wake with a start to realise that some
of them at least were death-sentences. You will, therefore, be well advised to accept with reserve his explanations of his residence in Ebury Street.

You would be equally well advised to accept with
reserve the account that he has given of himself in such
books as *Memoirs of my Dead Life,* or rather, perhaps,
of the legend that these books have caused to grow up
about him. George Moore is accused by his detractors
of posing, by his admirers of being perfectly natural.
Both are right, because he has achieved the artistically
natural, which is necessarily a pose, as, for example,
the attitude of Discobolus is a pose. Nature is a dis-
cordant mess; when left to itself it is wholly unnatural,
because wholly unaffected by the human mind. It becomes natural when the unity of mind and matter has
been effected. In George Moore at his best that unity
is almost completely achieved, and the result is the
classic pose of the figures in the Parthenon frieze.

There are two things to be said of that classic pose
which are universally true. The first is that it disturbs
all minds, and irritates many by arousing a sense of
inferiority. The second is that it is esentially an enigma.
The object of art is in itself to act as a signpost at a

cross-roads. The ways branch out in all directions. Emotions have come and gone, and worn the long lanes down. Some paths end in a bog, some find the sea, some lead to Babylon. But the signpost does not travel. It remains cold, and authoritative, pointing. It is for the traveller to make the journey.

In considering the account given by George Moore of his life, all this must be borne in mind. It must not be read like a trade-return, or as a statistical abstract, which goes without saying anything at all. The facts are in no sense objective; they are not, I mean, unconnected, chaotic, and therefore individually and in the mass insignificant. If the *Memoirs* were evidence tendered in a court of law, at least ten different verdicts might be pronounced on the character of the author. And they would all be wrong. Because there never was in the objective world such a young man as the George Moore of the narrative.

But, you may object, he gives actual names, places, and times. He does, and so should I if I said that on the 14th May, 1926, I took the mountain-train from Montreux to the Rochers de Naye. I could add that the day was so hot that the butterflies rested on and in the heat like fruit in a jelly. I could tell you that the train ploughed through flowers, like a ship cutting through a Pacific sea, where the foam fell back bright blue. I could say that there was nobody at the height, except me, a mist, and a lark, upon whose small brown back I meditatively gazed. I could conclude by observing that the innkeeper complimented me both on my hardihood and my appearance.

All that is true, and equally untrue. I have attempted to rescue from the million incidents that fill any four hours of any life a few that suggest how I should wish you to understand all the others. You may make any guess you choose about me from that fragment — that I am a poet, a nature-lover, a liar, a mountaineer, or a Cook's tourist. You may call the account a description of Switzerland, a picture-postcard, or journalism. But, trifling as it is, you will never overtake its poor little secret. Like all deliberate composition, it points beyond itself, and the facts assume long shadows.

If that is true of a few casual sentences, how far truer of a work of art such as the *Memoirs,* or still more of *Hail and Farewell*. The author is " making " always. He accepts from time only its shifting illusion in the necessary spatial shapes of " actual " events. The George Moore that emerges is as much a creation as the figure of Abélard in *Héloïse and Abélard*. The facts have the same reality — that of George Moore's mind. They have no other, because there could be none other.

If, therefore, we approach George Moore — the man — from this angle, the legend will appear for what it is — a tale, because of all writers in English George Moore is the supreme story-teller. I warned you at the beginning against accepting his explanations, if ever he gave them to you, of his residence in Ebury Street. I need hardly warn you against accepting my picture of him as historically accurate, or rather inaccurate. It is merely introduced to illustrate the fact that George Moore has by virtue of his great skill misled a literal world into taking him literally. He has been accused of a hundred things — spiritual flippancy, moral lightness, intellectual arrogance, and a habit of using his friends for copy. All these counts could be sustained in the court to which I have referred, if his work were put in as evidence against him. But in art there is no need for the police-constable of public opinion to warn the creator that anything he says will be used against him. It will not. It will be used against those who attempt so to pervert it.

Those, therefore, who engage in futile gossip about George Moore as a man write themselves down as so many Dogberrys. Let us suppose for a moment that the events described by Moore actually occurred. What, even then, do we know of all the events that, as far as our knowledge goes, didn't occur! What, in fact, do we know of the significance of a love-affair unless we ourselves took part in it? Nothing, or only that aspect of it which the writer chooses, for the purpose of his writing, to expose. What may appear to be the hall-mark of a libertine may in fact, if the whole circumstances were known, have been as tender (and ridiculous) as a Tennysonian idyll. Our business is with the work: not with the writer.

There are two reasons why George Moore more than other writers has suffered from tedious calumny.

The first is that brilliantly artful air of "the natural" which his simplicity of style evokes. "Good God!" gasps the reader, "but this is positively what happened. Heavens! What a wretch!" In fact, it is positively what couldn't have happened, because so finished an event never does happen. The second reason is that George Moore has something in his mind which corresponds to the width of his eyes. He does on occasion blurt out opinions, like a pleased child. He will say, for example, that education ought to be abolished, except for those who insist on getting it for themselves. Everything that is Puritan and restrictive in England puts up its hackles. But why? George Moore's opinions don't matter (whatever he may think). What does matter is the way in which they were expressed, and it is no doubt upsetting when odious or reactionary views are exhibited in faultless and permanent language. But that is no excuse for inventing malicious nonsense about a great writer. Let us concentrate on *The Brook Kerith* — a brook, as Housman might say, too broad for leaping by even the youngest of us.

But Mr. Moore does not want to talk about *The Brook* straight off. Have you noticed that nobody writes now, he says. The words are all stunned and stubborn, and the sentences have an earache. They don't want to tell stories, those fellows. They want to be reviewing the words as though it was a parade of soldiers. You can't do it that way. You have to be easy with the words, and they would be easy with you.

And remember that it is not the words that you're after, but the story. There was a young woman sent me a play that for writing wasn't at all bad. But the tale in it was wrong. There was a young man in it cured of a disease that wouldn't let him walk, and at the end of it he just walked out of the play. I wrote to her and said, "Let him walk into the girl's arms." But she would not, and the play failed. That's how it is with them. If they have words, they've no story, and if a story no style, but both they do not have. There's my little play now that the young American found in a drawer. It's nothing — just a light sketch — but it could be spoken, and it has as much tale as you would need to put salt on. I'm not sure, Mr. Moore, whether you or I made that last observation. I think that it probably belongs to me, but we won't quarrel about it. You shall have it. But the play is *The Making of an Immortal,* isn't it? With Burbage, and the eyasses, Will Shakespeare, Ben Jonson, and Belphœbe herself. It couldn't be acted, I think. It's too short by itself, and I don't see what you could play with it. Besides, Elizabeth only comes in for about five minutes, but her arrival is the crux of the play. You'd need a first-rate actress for the part, and you'd never get one for that little amount of talk. Then I don't believe you'd be able to get boys to play at all. You'd have to have young women for the company. I would not have young women. Their shapes would be all wrong, and their voices too. They must be lean like daffodils, not all

10

blown out like a peony. But I daresay you're right for the rest. There is more trouble with actors and actresses than there is in writing the play itself. But Gosse liked it so well that he asked could he have the manuscript to bind, and he had it. It was read, too, one evening at the house of Tonks, and they all liked it. I would, though, have let it be altogether, but for this young Wells that came round asking for something to have printed. There's the play in the drawer, Mr. Moore, Miss Kingdom said. It's been there these three years. Well, Mr. Wells, I said to him, here it is, if you want it. He was pleased enough. But it isn't about me or plays that I wanted to speak. It was why there was nobody writing tales now. It's too much to expect poetry, though I wouldn't say that de la Mare didn't write it. But prose is another thing. There are rules to it, of course, but, if they would be done with imitating God and counting the hairs of the heads of their characters, there'd be a chance. So much of their novels is like walking about in an analysed smell. Isn't Venus good enough for them that they've got to behave like a professor in the higher mathematics? That would be James Joyce you're speaking of, or Mrs. Woolf, Mr. Moore. You'll admit, I suppose, that even if Joyce wrote *Ulysses* as though he were Calypso in a thunderstorm, the *Portrait of the Artist as a Young Man* is both writing and a story. I don't pretend to know what *Ulysses* is intended to convey either to Joyce or the reader. It does seem to me as though it were the dictionary in

the throes of a Bolshevist revolution, with the pro-
nouns as Commissars and all the verbs decapitated as
aristocrats. But, after all, it's real revolution. You mayn't
like revolutions, but you can't deny them. I'm not
denying them, my dear Wolfe. But you don't produce
a revolution in literature by banishing sense to Siberia.
I suppose that I'm as much an anarchist in life as most
men — though perhaps I brag about it less. But if I
want to draw a picture of an anarchist, I don't show
him at the moment that he's just been blown up by a
bomb. Look at the Post-Impressionists. You may say
they believed in the democracy of colour. But they
didn't stand any nonsense about self-determination
when it came to the canvas. In the beginning, the Bible
says, was the void. There is still, but the Creator was
an artist, and nobody would guess it, looking superficially at the world. It's only when you begin to concentrate that you find that its arrangement imposed
from outside on what is permanently disorderly. That's
how it would be with Esther Waters. I wasn't thinking that a servant-maid was like a girl painted in a
Hogarth picture, all fixed with her white mutch. I
let her in looking so, because it wouldn't be decent
else. But there's the whole dissolution of life behind
her. The tale has got to get itself told in them that
live in it. The significance is in the life itself. You can't
put it in from without, any more than you can put
the smell in a rose by listening to a nightingale. No,
but you can, can't you, help the smell by manuring the

12

ground, and watering the rose in the dry season. You don't just plant a seed and then go off to the Canaries for a holiday. You can even change the rose from a briar to a Glory of Dijon if you're the right sort of gardener. You wouldn't do less for life, I imagine, in a novel. Not less I wouldn't, but no more. I wouldn't begin with nothing at all and expect to be able to make a rose-pergola with it. I would have my bits of men and women, and how they grew and changed and died would be their affairs. I'd see to it that the style gave them fair play. That's how I had such trouble with *The Brook Kerith*. It's queer the way you picked on the passage of Jesus wandering across the hills, looking for the ram for the flock and bringing it back in his arms. For that was one thing I never could write, or would have written, if I had not gone to Palestine. You remember it, don't you? I remember it, Mr. Moore. When He had recovered after the Crucifixion, Joseph of Arimathea took Him back to the monastery of the Essenes. He was skilled with flocks, and so the head of the monastery put Him back to shepherd the flock, almost wasted away for want of a young ram. He found his ram-lamb after a long search in the bleak hills, and brought him back in His arms, when both of them were in danger of perishing with hunger and thirst. It seemed to me, when I read it, of all commentaries on the Gospel the most poignant. Here was the Good Shepherd of all the world almost losing His life to save, not mankind, but a little flock of sheep in the hills of Palestine. How often have we not seen the picture of the Shepherd with the lamb in His arms, and here was the same picture, painted with the halo changed into a cloud of daily human effort and suffering? It was as though Mona Lisa had explained that the smile, of which Pater wrote, was only a nervous twitch. For me that would have heightened, rather than reduced, the mystery. Because Pater wanted a picture to prove a theory, but I had rather that it disproved one. Yes, but if you could write like Pater, you'd be entitled to ask that, or more, of a picture. There, if you like, was style, ornate, encrusted like a goblet and teased out, but still style. I remember when Pater — But please don't remember about Pater just now, or you'll make me say (what probably Oscar Wilde said before me) that Pater's writing wasn't living prose, but prose lying in state. And, if I said that, we should get away from *The Brook Kerith,* which is so much more important that Pater, and any first- or second-hand witticisms of mine. Yes, but wait a minute, please. If it is yours, though I don't agree with it, it's a first-rate criticism in four words. It would almost make me believe that you could write, if you'd say such things. As long as you don't read my verse, you mean, Mr. Moore. Ah, well! but, in any case, it probably was Oscar who said it, or Whistler, or York-Powell, or all three or each one claimed it. But do let's get back to our ram-lamb. Why has that particular passage such a significance? Was it because you felt you had in a single pic-

14

ture, sternly and economically drawn, offered a criticism of a thousand years of faith? Nothing of the kind, my dear Wolfe. Won't you young men ever understand that writing isn't preaching, nor controversy, nor yet rhapsody, but the plain and unembroidered way of telling a story. If I were to build a house, would I be proud, d'you think, if, instead of being inhabited, it was taken to be a proof of the Fifth Proposition in *Euclid?* A house is a house, if the architect knows his business, and a tale is a tale — just that and no more. If I'd thought that the episode of Jesus and the ram-lamb was a symbol, or a comment, or a proof, or anything irrelevant whatever, I'd have had it cut out, as I've cut out twenty scenes and more that might have charm in them, but hurt the tale. There's a whole story in *Héloïse and Abélard* — of Peronnik, the Fool — that I wouldn't put in, and after published by itself. I'm not saying that a tale doesn't some time call for a digression, but argument or views of the author's are not that. They're just ignorance of his art. But, Mr. Moore, you've called your novels philosophical, haven't you? That means — if it means anything — that they are, if not an explanation of or comment on life, at least a point of view. I confess that I don't see how any author can escape imposing his point of view. However objective he seeks to be, his loves and hates, preconceptions and prejudices, must colour his story. You can't imagine Thomas Hardy writing *Travels with a Donkey* or Robert Louis Stevenson *Jude the Obscure.*

I can't imagine Thomas Hardy writing anything, Wolfe, nor Stevenson being such a fool as to get himself lost between sentences which are like an Irish bog and a man walking there in boots for climbing the Alps. Of course, the author has a point of view, but it should be a point of view of people, not of things. He takes figures out of the Human Comedy or Tragedy, and lets them live it out according to the truth or the untruth that is in them. I shouldn't myself see my men and women growing up and out like what they would in Balzac or Flaubert. Perhaps even my people wouldn't be on speaking terms with " La Vieille Fille " and Madame Bovary. But they'd know one another for inhabitants of the same world. Balzac's and Flaubert's were very different characters from mine, and they looked for different reactions in their creations. But they wouldn't set out to show that two straight lines couldn't enclose a space, any more than I would. That's art — to make your own attitude no more than a legitimate expectation. I wish that we had the time, Mr. Moore, to explore that conclusion of yours. It would, for example, put eighty per cent. of H. G. Wells out of court, and seriously undermine the claims of a whole modern school of writers. On the other hand, it would provide a defence both of *Ulysses* and *To the Lighthouse*. Though perhaps you would say that both Joyce and Virginia Woolf permitted expectation to dwindle into a vague, undigested hope that something might perhaps happen to somebody somewhere. And, " Good God! " they might justly say at the end of their book, " I'm not sure that it has." It's a slow-motion picture, so slow that, if you reproduce a man walking, all you've seen is the slow expansion of one muscle, and in Joyce's case a scrap of dirty shin. But, if we pursue that, we shall forget *The Brook Kerith* and that you went to Palestine. I think that I'd rather hear the reasons of the journey even than for the moment discuss the fundamental principles of story-telling. Well, my dear Wolfe, the truth about *The Brook* is that years ago I'd had the present of a Bible. I think it was John Eglinton with whom I first spoke of writing the story of Jesus. It was at evening, I think, when I spoke of it with him, years before I came to the writing of it. I thought, of course, of Joseph of Arimathea in his father's house, because there would have to be some other figure than that of Jesus to carry the weight of the tale. I thought then of the life of the young man Joseph by the Lake, of the Romans, of Tiberias, of the journeys to Jerusalem. Then when I thought of Jesus I had to conceive the life of the Essene monastery, of the road to the mountains, and how the buildings would be crouched like an Italian hill-church, clinging to the skin of the rocks over a drop of a thousand feet. I thought of it, but all the time I was disturbed by ignorance of the locality. If I wanted Joseph to walk to Tiberias, how far would that be, and could he do it in a day and be back home with his teacher by evening? Or if Joseph searched for Jesus and found

Him walking by the way, what sort of a way would it be He'd be walking? Or if a monk stood on the terrace looking out into the day, what hills would he be seeing — low mounds of rolling mud, or tall and angry green mountains? And if there were yowes to be herded, how would they be pastured and how folded? I had none of these things in my mind, and I knew that I wouldn't write the tale until I'd seen all with my own eyes. I don't want to interrupt, but it's curious, Mr. Moore, that you'd need the bare facts. There is a young writer — Ronald Fraser — who wrote a novel on a Chinese theme — *Landscape with Figures* — and all the China he'd ever seen was a willow-pattern plate. It was a good novel, and if China isn't like what he imagined, it ought to be. Imagination, Humbert Wolfe, goes a long way, but you mustn't ride it to death. If there are no facts and it has to carry the whole weight, it begins to flag, and the power of the author, that should be directed to the tale, suffers. I don't mean the writer must have the whole of Bradshaw by heart before he can describe a railway journey from Waterloo to Surbiton. But he ought at least to have seen a train, and, if possible, to have spoken to a porter. Anyway, that's how it is with me, and that's how I went to Palestine. It was from Jerusalem that I made the two journeys — one to find the place for the monastery of the Essenes, the other to the Lake of Galilee to come by a knowledge of how the merchants, the fishermen, and the Romans would be living by the side of it. I rode out from Jerusalem on a little hard horse — eight hours the ride was — and starting before dawn. Neither could we stop by the way, because there was a bitter, hot valley of stones that we had to cross, and no place to shelter in the mid-day heat. Early in the ride we passed by a stream that cuts its way through a gully. They told me, when I asked, it was called the Brook of the Chariots. Were they the chariots of the Lord, I wondered, that had a way cloven through the hills, or had the Romans splashed through it with the great, heavy, studded wheels. I found later that both guesses were wrong. It was the Brook Kerith that I'd misheard the name of, and, though I didn't know it then, here were the head-waters of my tale. You can guess that I grew saddlesore in that bitter land open to the sun. I'd have fallen off the horse if they hadn't had me tied to it with my legs below the belly of him. It was well into the afternoon when we saw a sharp rise in the hills, and there, sticking to a rock the way it had been a fly stuck to a paper, a little high building. "That is the monastery," said my guide. "How do we get to it?" I asked. "By the path," he said, showing me a road fastened into the brown earth as clean as a cork-screw fastened into a cork. There were precipices on the side of it, and my guide rode it easily. But I made him untie me, and stumbled up, holding on by the tail of the beast. We knocked at the monastery and they came out to us. They were monks of a Greek order and had no English or French, and I had to make do with what Greek and interpretation could give. I wanted to know by what way, if the yowes of the monastery grazed on the hills, they could be brought home. Was there some hole or tunnel in the heights through which they could be driven? I needed that, you see, if I was to have the picture of Jesus bringing home his flock. The guide seemed to understand and make himself understood. Tired as we were, we toiled up the sheer hill. We reached, after long climbing, a knoll which, I finally gathered, represented some tradition in Old Testament history. But that wasn't what I needed. We continued clambering in the sultry evening, till we came to a point where the conditions I required for the folding of the flocks were fulfilled. Drenched with fatigue to the bone, I returned to the monastery and tumbled, like an empty sack, into sleep in the cold cell. It was still early when I woke. I went out on to the terrace in front of the monastery, and looked over the countryside in which I was to live while I wrote the book. I will not describe it. It is in the book. All I need tell you is that I cried to my own eyes, "I beseech you, remember! For you will never look upon all this again." We rode back that day to Jerusalem. I rested for a few days, and then made my other pilgrimage to Galilee. I had suffered Palestine then in my own body and my own sweat. I came back to Ebury Street no longer a stranger in the land of the Scripture, and I began to write.

As I walked back from Ebury Street through the rain of a February afternoon, I compared the portrait that Mr. Moore had, with no ulterior object, given of himself as a craftsman with that which some casual readers had derived from his autobiographical books. The second (and wholly false) picture represented him as a deliberate stylist, for whom life had only a secondary importance. It is suggested, too, that there was in the easy droop of the hand an intellectual indolence that was content to scratch a glass surface. The instrument, it is true, was a diamond, but not even a precious stone could give depth, or even permanence, to what was, after all, scrawled lightly on a transparent and brittle ground. They would say, these portraitists, that he didn't even look out at life through the window while he worked with his diamond, but felt that life was lucky to have a chance of looking in at him. They would perhaps even suggest that ultimately he was only half-serious, saying, as Scott said of Byron, that he always wrote with the pen of a gentleman.

And yet even without Mr. Moore's own account of his pilgrimage to Mecca, they could and should have seen from the books themselves — notably from *Hail and Farewell* — that, whatever else their subject might not be, he was a craftsman who had achieved his eminence by sheer grinding hard work. They could not, of course, know that he would re-write a page as often as Plato re-wrote the first sentences of *The Republic*. But they had the mere bulk of his production on the one hand, and on the other the even perfection of the writing. Was it reasonable to suppose that any man had been secretly given by the Muse that effortless certainty of word-control? Was it possible that the apparent artlessness, with which the whole work moved to its conclusion, was the result of repeated accident? And, even apart from the supreme literary competence, was it to be imagined that Mr. Moore had acquired the sure contemporary grasp of the periods of Jesus and Abélard without labour, or application?

The contrary is, of course, the case. Mr. Moore as a literary artisan is a monk of letters. There is nothing he will not demand of himself in the pursuit of his object. He will not only wear out his body in Palestine, but he will wear out his heart over a single sentence. A man of over seventy years of age, he sat down again to *The Brook Kerith* and, as he said, re-orchestrated it. No better education could be afforded to a student of letters than to examine the penultimate and the last edition, and to learn from a textual study what Mr. Moore means by re-orchestration. Such a student would find hardly a page in which some word had not been altered, withdrawn, or added. He would find in one or two places passages of real beauty omitted. If the student put all the amendments and alterations together, he would conclude that Mr. Moore's one object was to clear out of the way any obstruction, however small, which might impede the development of the tale. He wants no picturesque pools in the brook, no romantic little eddies. He does not want it to babble, to make sudden rushes, to be coy and go on, like

Tennyson's, repeating itself for ever, while men, who unguardedly come, naturally go. He means it to flow evenly, clearly, and strongly to its distant and certain home " of waters wide." He clears the channel of stones, as he clears it sometimes of the overhanging (but still obstructing) beauties of willow and long grasses. His brook is to have no adventitious aids. It must convince by its own merit, the merit of cool water drawn, and drawing by the impulse of its own strength, to the Jordan.

If we contemplate that picture, we shall have a very different portrait to set against the first. We shall discover in Mr. Moore one of the few writers who has ever added cubits to his stature by taking thought. It is as possible to say of the author of *Memoirs of my Dead Life,* even of the author of *Esther Waters,* that here is great talent, but talent that has not bitten into life. It is barely possible even to suggest that of the author of *The Brook Kerith* and *Abélard.* If we use the first image, Mr. Moore is still working with a diamond, but it is in bronze that he is working, and cutting very deep. We see him, therefore, as a man who has never yielded an inch either to popular taste or to critical fashions. He has set before himself the ideal of " pure " art, art that is wholly objective. He has refined his gold in crucible after crucible, and it has emerged cleaner, finer, and harder after each test.

Where, then, is the Mr. Moore of the *Confessions?*

There is such a Mr. Moore, a man who has not attempted to conceal his tastes and distastes in life. He has loved Cynara after his fashion, and he tells us so. It is neither a boast nor an apology. He treats himself as objectively when he writes as he treated Joseph of Arimathea. The only difference is that he has more facts. But when he comes to set them down he insists on their right to develop themselves as freely as the facts in *The Brook*. He does not ask to be liked or disliked, any more than did Benvenuto Cellini. Each of them — Moore and Cellini — were craftsmen, and they could not conceive of themselves as other than objects of their art. It is a matter of indifference to both that the world may say of them, " But this was a buccaneer." Their answer is, " That can't be helped. This is how it was. We can none other."

And so I come back to George Moore lying in bed at the nursing-home, when he was in daily expectation of a life-and-death operation. He was far more ill than he knew, and, as sick men will, grumbled more than a little. Death, he said, he didn't mind, but this business of dying was in the last degree tedious. Even so, when every word cost him an effort, he spoke with the old fire of literature. His play *The Making of an Immortal* was to be produced. He contrived to be as fierce about dramatic rectitude as though he were a young man who had never known that compromise was the name that the English give to artistic experience. He refused any concession. The play must be acted as he saw it, or not at all. And it was so acted, with what success the world knows.

But, to set beside this picture of the formidable and relentless artist, there is this other. He has been spoken of as a man of poses, as a man like Heine, having every-thing except love, as in the last degree devoid of sim-plicity. He was very tired one evening. He had been in continuous pain for weeks, and he was borne down by the long, empty hours in the nursing-home. He spoke of getting away for a short holiday by the Seine, to the places he had known when he was an art-student in Paris. And then he said, "I want a few quiet things now: my room in Ebury Street, and just to be sitting talking with you by the fire again — just quiet things like that."

THE CRAFT OF VERSE

The Craft of Verse

I WAS sitting on the terrace in front of the Grand Hotel at St. Cergue, wondering whether Mont Blanc had gone too far by anticipating the arrangement which the mind seeks to impose on the object, when, to my surprise, I heard a familiar voice calling to me from between the pines a hundred feet below. This was R. — a leader of the modern poets — who, entirely unknown to me, had invaded my Swiss territories. Undeterred by my forbidding manner, he climbed up the steep slope accompanied by Artur Delarue — a French poet — whom I had met and distrusted in Paris. They settled themselves by my side on the seat, and, without any adequate explanation or apology, addressed themselves to criticism of the scene. They were agreed that it was faulty, but could not agree as to the nature of the faults. R. was not disposed to quarrel with the composition, which, though traditional, was at least sincere. He was prepared to admit that a more audacious mind would at least have omitted the lake, or have dispensed with the decoration afforded by the pine-woods. But there was evidence of thought, if often superficial. His complaint was that the thing was too direct.

R.: Here, said he (and at this point I may perhaps be permitted the liberty of direct speech) — here is an artist of considerable ability ruining his work by leaving nothing to anybody else's imagination, and very little in his own. He is entitled to use mountains, or a lake, or the massed and marching pines. But he need not have insisted on a range so vast, so white, so sunlit, so popularly and objectively a mountain. He need not have thrown in, without analysis, so coolly perfect, so decoratively surrounded a water. Nor on this day is it necessary to repeat the snow effects in the clouds, nor to offer a mountain-echo in heaven. What is presented to the eye is the abundant raw material for a scene rather than the selected result. The Creator should have set aside this first rough sketch. He should, over a period, then have brooded on the essential details. He should, for example, have asked himself, "What is the essence of a mountain?" He should not have accepted the common formula of trees, rocks, glacier, moraine, and incontrovertible snows. He should (and, having regard to his obvious talent, could) have reduced all this to a personal — and therefore possibly permanent — expression which would suggest all these traditional objects without, perhaps, ever using them at all. He might, and should have, modified the undigested romance by some indication of the fallibility of all human appreciation of beauty. He might have introduced a series of coal-pits into the foreground, or substituted West Ham for the lake. It is plain that

30

what he has, in fact, done is not to give us a true object of sight, but a thing which we believe that we see, because a million others equally astigmatic have shared that belief. And all this criticism applies equally to verse. I —

D.: Before you develop the argument in that direction, I may perhaps be permitted to indicate where I think your otherwise justifiable indignation is at fault. It is true that all this is vulgar, a violent reaffirmation of exactly what artistic truth is not, and never has been. But I do not think that you have sufficiently explored the metaphysics of the crime that we are witnessing. There are two possible ways of approaching reality — the completely subjective, and the entirely objective, though I am not prepared to deny that at some points the two are identical. It will, I suppose, be admitted that all sight is a conspiracy between the eye and the object. Reality is a just distribution of the result between the two. For example, when I look at that mountain I think of the pain in my legs induced by climbing. I remember a Japanese (and extremely tawdry) representation of their holy mountain, like the ice-cream they will always give you in the *voiture*-restaurant. I think of the two francs ten of which that abominable tobacconist at Nyon cheated me; and I must write to my publishers, denying that the proofs have reached me. Obviously, therefore, if my half of the business of seeing is to be fairly represented, some allowance must be made for all these mixed impressions. On the other side, it is fair to suppose that the mountain too has its transient idiosyncrasies. It is, of course, not possible to represent them in terms of thought, but a token might quite reasonably be adopted, such as is afforded by arbitrary patterns. The true combination would, therefore, be a fusion of my fleeting impressions with appropriately grouped mountain symbols or patterns. And, if that be true in respect of one human mind, how much truer in respect of the presumably larger entity who precipitated this romantic superficiality with which he seeks to debauch us. What incomparable irrelevancies must occupy the intellect of the Ancient of Days: what fertile chaos, what glimpses of wrecked Edens, sacked Assyrian cities, gusts of passion, fear, and illimitable fatigue. He should have given us a hint of all that, and, since he claims to have invented the mountain, he should at least have understood its pattern. In short, he prefers journalism to art, as in verse he would have preferred so hopeless a reactionary as Paul Valéry to some such comparatively enlightened performer as Blaise Cendras.

MYSELF: It is obliging of you, R., to have brought your friend to relieve my boredom. Before your arrival I was attempting to curb my own notorious romanticism, and had even humbly doubted whether I was justified in accepting all that Mont Blanc was so wantonly offering. I confess that, if I had been denied the privilege of your company, I might have actually given way. I might have justified my weakness by urging on myself that to work in the open and in the grand manner may not necessarily be a sign of debility. I might even have been betrayed into the conjecture that thus Shakespeare, if he had had the universe instead of words for his medium, might have transacted business. And how wrong (it seems) I should have been! I should have confused (it appears) bravado with courage, violence with strength — unless indeed, as is possible, you, Delarue, think I should rightly have made this assumption in respect of Shakespeare, whom you may regard as the supreme traitor to beauty. Or possibly you have not read his works?

D.: I must beg you to treat serious things seriously. R. and I were considering the principles of art, and we will not be deterred by your habitual flippancy. Let us, if you please, for once dispense with wit.

Myself: Certainly, let us be as dull as possible. But since, as I understand it, wit is a fundamental and sudden arrangement of the chaotic, and laughter the mind's verdict upon it, I can promise you to be monotonous, though, alas! nothing can make me profound. But before R. adds his reprimand to yours, I should like to take one point in your disquisition, and apply it to the craft of verse, which is, of course, at the back of both your minds.

I shall not follow you, Delarue, into the metaphysic

of pure art which I believe you to have been attempting. I will congratulate you on the courage with which you assert that you have solved it. You have, as I understand it, substituted for Descartes' "*Cogito ergo sum*" some formula such as "I can't think clearly, therefore reality must be confusion." But I pass from that to the consideration of your theory of patterns.

You assert that, since we cannot hope to understand the object, we ought to substitute an arbitrary pattern to represent its possible reactions, and you scold the Creator for having used a mountain-pattern to convey a mountain. That suggests to me a flaw at the base of your reasoning. Because, in fact, the mountain is actually an arbitrary pattern, and it is only because you have become habituated to it that it seems to you traditional. In the same way all verse-patterns — even down to the fantastic triolet — are arbitrary and astonishing in themselves. It is this simple fact which constantly escapes the innovator. He will not realise that the object is always the same, it is only the mind that you bring to it that changes.

R.: If you carry your proposition to its logical issue, you would be bound to conclude that all possible verse-forms existed when the first tribal bard attempted diluted cacophonies. But surely exactly the opposite is the truth. Each period of genuine verse-production evolves, not only its own approach to the object, but its own object. The primitive form is naturally narrative, as in

34

the ballads and sagas, rising in the case of high genius to an *Iliad* or a "Romaunt de Rolland." Even at that stage you have the widest differences. The Greek genius evolves out of its own ringing shapeliness the hexameter. The early French expresses itself in assonance, and the English in alliteration. There is no common point, except the common desire to tell a tale.

D.: Yes, and we may pursue that point further by observing that the true creative impulse in each period not only seeks, but consists in, a new form as well as a new content. Consider what happens when an attempt is made to use the narrative form appropriate to an earlier period in a later. You have in Rome poor Vergil, Lucan, Statius, and their even duller successors, turning out long-winded turgidities which are neither tales nor poetry. You have all the dreary ballads of the Middle Ages, and you have your Milton redeemed from sensational failure by reason of the fact that the wine he poured into the old bottle of the epic burst it, and soaked into the earth in a thousand lyrical shapes. It is only when the old Milton writes in the manner of the author of *L'Allegro* that he is a poet — though naturally, as each nation insists, as a matter of pride, on having one epic poet, the English cannot be expected to admit this.

Myself: Your argument would, I think, be more effective if it did not lead to results incompatible with the long judgments of the centuries. There is, of course, no reason, if you have, in fact, read Vergil, why you should not personally dislike him. But if your theory begins by requiring the world at large to share that view, it is, I think, the theory rather than Vergil that will be discredited. But we had better go a little further back, and ask ourselves what it is that the poet sets out to do which distinguishes him from the other artists in words. If we can discover an answer to that question, we may perhaps make some advance to a general theory. If, for example, we conclude that a poet must express himself, not only differently from all writers in prose, but from all other poets — at any rate, poets not of his generation — we shall have done something to support your theory. If, on the other hand, we find that the sonnet can be written with success and beauty by Petrarch, Shakespeare, Ronsard, Wordsworth, and Swinburne, we may have to revise our premises.

D.: The sonnet will prove nothing. It is not a form of poetry, but a gaol in which poetry, condemned to a life-sentence, naturally loses its individuality. It should have been burned with the Bastille, and indeed, in the process of the new revolution, we are burning it.

MYSELF: No doubt the flames will illuminate your own successes. But I think that we shall be begging the preliminary question if we rule out any form of verse which has, in the opinion of many, justified itself beyond question. Let us, if we may, therefore return to the original mutton that I asked you to brand.

R.: We cannot brand it, as you know, or should know perfectly well. You can ask, as a matter of history or evolution, how the poet came to be so distinguished. But, since his ultimate development is a matter of conjecture, any conclusion would be the merest empiricism.

D.: Emphatically, since poetry is only a way of writing prose.

MYSELF: So I observe in much of current practice. But I have sometimes permitted myself to wonder whether those who took that view were not like the naked king in the fairy-tale, suffering much, in addition to other inconveniences, from wind. Let me, at any rate, observe that, if we begin by asserting that there is, in fact, no distinction between verse and prose, we have gone a long way in defining the craft of verse. We shall be able to dispense, from the outset, with rhyme, formal rhythm, rules of prosody, and maintain that poetry is never in the form but only in the substance of what is written.

We might, for example, publish the advertisement columns of a newspaper in the way that lyrics have often been published, one to a page, with a healthy margin. That would at least save a certain amount of trouble.

R.: We have asked you before to be serious.

MYSELF: But I am serious. You remember the old salt in Stevenson's parable who smoked in the powder-magazine of a sinking ship? I haven't the book here, so I can only quote from memory. The startled Captain, coming upon him, rebuked him. The sailor, however, objected that, as the ship was sinking, he didn't see the difference between going on with his functions or smoking in the powder-magazine. " Or," said the Captain, now thoroughly convinced, "doing anything whatever in any conceivable circumstances. Perfectly conclusive — give me a cigar." Two minutes later the ship blew up with a glorious detonation. I was merely, with the same severe logic, helping poetry to the same conclusion. The trouble, you see, with innovators is that they regard logic as reactionary. When, therefore, I carry Delarue's contention to its natural conclusion, you combine in accusing me of flippancy.

D.: I daresay, my dear R., that he is serious, and that his seriousness supplies the secret of his own versification, which has hitherto escaped me. But, my dear Wolfe, if there is a distinction between poetry and prose, which I deny, it is for you as the champion to defend its title.

38

R.: I am not sure, Delarue, that I can go all the way with you. We must admit, I think, that a poet gives words a function not exercised when a writer of prose marshals them. If this were not so, why, for example, do you describe your own work as verse, and why do we distinguish in the case of the Anglo-American writer, Eliot — whom we both admire — his verse and his criticism? It cannot be subject-matter only. Horace, for example, wrote his criticism in verse, as, I believe, Boileau did with you. Wolfe, I think, is right in believing that there is a distinction, though we should probably agree in rejecting the grounds upon which he draws it. But, at any rate, he had better attempt to let us have them.

Myself: I cannot see that I am called upon to make the distinction. I am entitled to rely upon the facts. If a metaphysician denies the distinction between dreaming and waking, I say to him, "Very well, you deny a universally shared and shareable belief. It is for you to substitute one as universal." I do not begin by defending dreams. They speak for themselves. *Que messieurs les assassins commencent.*

D.: I thought that we should find him running away when he was put to it. "These things exist," he cries, with true reactionary fervour, "therefore they are." He begs the question, you observe, of their existence. But since he refuses, I will restate what is a platitude to all students of evolution. I begin by asserting that there is only one shape in every species which adapts itself to progressive environment. Thus man is post-Triassic monkey, a whale is a large cow that lost its feet by being compelled to stand for several thousand centuries in shallow water to avoid the assaults of even larger and less docile beasts, and so through all creation. When we apply this doctrine to the principles of art there is a reasonable certainty that it provides an epistemological basis. It is, I think, generally admitted that verse precedes prose in point of time, and that is natural. Primitive man, devoid of the higher facilities of reason, and unable to write, expresses himself rudely and supports his rugged failures by having resort to mnemonics. These take the form of stampings and loud, moaning inflections which develop into metre and rhythm. That is the legitimate origin of these meretricious ornaments. But as his mind develops, and, above all, when he discovers the secret of the alphabet, he throws aside these toys, and turns naturally to prose. He expresses in that medium all that could be, and far more than actually was, possible in the clumsier primitive mode. He is no longer subject to the whims of scansion and stress. He is not a slave to rules having no intrinsic value but invented purely as aids to memory. He can now speak all out with the gravity, the leisure, the innumerable subtleties, and, above all, the natural flow of prose. He is not governed by a catch in the breath, or by the fallibility of the ear. He can direct

40

himself to that nobler and stricter organ, the eye. In a word, he is out of prison.

If an illustration were needed I could take no more conclusive a comparison than that afforded by Homer and Thucydides. I do not enter on the vexed question whether Homer was the name of a man or of a period. That is immaterial for my purpose. All that concerns me here is that what is called Homer is early in date, and was composed at a period when current writing, at any rate, had not been invented. The author, or authors, had therefore no alternative but to use for the purpose of their history the barbaric inelegancies of the hexameter. These corresponded in their stress to the thud of naked feet in a primitive dance, or to the rubbing of rude drums. It may perhaps be assumed that the *Iliad* and *Odyssey* were conceived, not as fairy-tales, but as actual chronicles of traditional events. From that angle, see how the unfortunate performers were harassed by their medium. Consider the endless repetition of epithets — "αμυμων," "εὐδειελος," "ποδας ωκυς" (to cite the few that I remember after this passage of time) — or still more the blatant repetition of phrases and lines. These were clearly the subterfuges of mediocre intellects marking time while they tried to think of something to say. And these are not the only inconveniences imposed by the form. The noise, like crepitations of a jazz band, go to the writer's head, with the result that he indulges in wanton poeticisms, irrelevancies which in a cooler moment or at a more reasonable period he would certainly have rejected. What could be less tolerable than the conversation between Achilles and the immortal horses? Achilles' proper business was to look to their grooming and accoutrements, and not to bandy words with quadrupeds on eschatology.

MYSELF: In which, I may interrupt, you charmingly remind me of Bentley's criticism of the last lines of *Paradise Lost*. They are, you remember:

> *. . . with wandering steps and slow*
> *Through Eden took their solitary way.*

He pointed out that Adam and Eve, being under the supervision (indeed under the close supervision) of their Creator, could not be described as solitary, and went on to observe that in these circumstances their steps, so far from being wandering and slow, would have been distinguished by a certain brisk alertness. He suggested, indeed, textual amendments to that effect. In the same way —

R.: For Heaven's sake do not be facetious. I don't in the least agree with what Delarue is saying, but it is worth respectful attention. We can both take our turn when he has finished his argument.

MYSELF: I apologise for Bentley. Continue, Delarue, but do not forget that some time or another we shall need lunch. There is, they tell me, a quite astonishing trout of the lake, which I have bespoken.

D.: I will not forget the trout — nor for once, R., do I think that Wolfe's interposition was altogether meaningless. Bentley, though he did not know it, was, in his textual chastisement of Milton, objecting to the fact that he had used a completely unsuitable vehicle. But I return to my Greeks. Thucydides, like Homer, had a story to tell which, since it is history, would be no less fictitious than the *Iliad*. But, unlike the ancient, he was absolutely unfettered —

MYSELF: Except by the rules of Greek syntax.

D.: Which were, in fact, beaten paths through the wilderness of ignorance. In these happy circumstances he could walk at his leisure, he could group, and, above all, he could select. When he described the mutilation of the Hermæ, for example, he had not to adapt his account to the demands of the dactyl. He had escaped for ever from the tyranny of toys. He was out of the nursery. The result is that his history can be read with pleasure and respect, and at its best moment with exactly the emotions which are commonly associated with poetry. At the end of the VII Book, when he had described the downfall of Athens, his dear city, at the conclusion of the Sicilian side-show he remarks, "Ταυτα δ' ἐγενετο ἐν τῃ Σικελιᾳ." Was there ever an emotion as poignant, as inevitable, when some pale-faced slave burst in on Priam with the fatal news of burning Ilion? No! the boasted province of verse had been invaded, over-run, and despoiled, and the greater victor sat calm and splendid in the pitiful ruins.

And I am prepared to maintain that that is universally true of the relation of verse and prose. Man lisps in numbers because the numbers come: he speaks in units.

R.: You would conclude, therefore, that poetry is only one brand of prose, or would you not even allow it a separate entity? Would you distinguish at all between two such works as Joyce's *Ulysses* and Eliot's *Waste-Land?* For purposes of convenience at least, they are separately classified, and I should have thought that there was so marked a difference both in object and effect as to constitute one, not of degree, but of kind.

D.: I recognise no distinction. The effect (and it seems to me the object) of what is best in both works are to me identical. The succession of jerked-out " yeses " in the last page of *Ulysses* has exactly the same value as so perfect a line as:

The nightingale cries jug-jug to dirty ears.

Indeed, the truth probably is that to-day prose is the name that we give to our mistakes in poetry. Or, not to borrow Wolfe's manner, one might say simply that poetry is simply prose at its best.

44

Thus, *Waste-Land* may be regarded as the chapter-headings in a library on ethnology. It is, in fact, an encyclopædia on the origins and decay of life. Eliot realised that each line must be the headline for a volume, and, by so constituting it, would become poetry. Joyce wrote not only the headlines, but the chapters as well. That was, perhaps, a pity.

R.: And yet I am not wholly convinced even by your history. Let me take your instance both of the monkeys and Greece. There may indeed be one aboriginal species from which both men and monkeys sprang. But the fact remains that at the moment both survive.

D.: That, my dear R., is no excuse for the monkey. He merely adds obstinacy to ignorance — which is my complaint against poetical poets.

R.: And yet, Delarue, Euripides — no mean performer — was contemporary with Thucydides. Catullus is of Cicero's period. You may prefer Thucydides to Euripides, or Cicero to Catullus (though remember poor old Tully had a shot at hexameters!), but I think you will have to explain the unshakable persistence of verse. You may call the poet the monkey of letters, but you will not get rid of him by abusing him.

MYSELF: Any more than you get rid of the monkey-house at the Zoo by building yourself a House of Parliament. You cannot, I mean, say the best monkeys are men, because there are certain admirable things possible to monkeys denied to men. What would I not give to be able to swing down through those firs from branch to branch in a green, leaf-lit curve. And " don't you envy their pranceful hands, don't you wish you had extra hands? " You cannot, I think, be certain what purpose, if any, gave us both men and monkeys, and I really do not see by what standards you prefer one to another.

But my quarrel with you, Delarue, is that, on your own assumptions, you do not go too far, but not far enough. I have been reading lately the translation by Mr. F. S. Flint and Miss D. F. Tait of René Fülöp-Miller's book on *Bolshevism*. The book devoted five or six most illuminating chapters to the theory of art evolved by that political movement. I happen to have by me, because I wrote it out at the time, the definition of verse advanced by a certain Shershen 'evich in a pamphlet entitled *Twice Two are Five*. " The image," says this leader of mechanism in verse, " entirely unconnected with other images is our object, the image *per se;* a poetical work which contains a ' leading image,' that is, an image to which all the others are subordinate and with which they are interwoven, does not exist for us. The image as such is subject and content. It must form a self-contained unit, since any combination of individual images is a mechanical and not an organic work. A poem is not an organism, but a heaping-up of images, any of which can be removed without loss, just as twenty new ones may be introduced. Only if each unit is complete, is the result a readable whole. I am firmly convinced that a book ought to be readable backwards as successfully as the other way round, just as a picture of Iakulov or Edimann may be hung upside down without loss."

Here, Delarue, are thinkers who have gone the whole way. For them, as for you, there can be no distinction between verse or prose, or at most an easily ascertainable arithmetical distinction. Lines, we are perhaps safe in assuming, containing not more than a given number of words are verse; the longer are prose. And both have the same object, which is to let isolated words speak for themselves. Art must be concrete and mechanical to the last degree; no indulgence may be permitted to individual fancy or genius. Given a dictionary and a revolutionary mind, all that is necessary is to dismiss words with any tradition, and then at random chemically to combine the others. There is no reason, therefore, why verse should not be sold over the counter according to requirements, provided naturally that the requirements are collective and not individual.

R.: Is it really relevant to deluge us with this nonsense? The moment that art is distorted to serve political purposes it loses its meaning. Why waste time on the Bolshevists, who are no more to blame or to be praised than any King in history who directed the activities of his Court Poet.

MYSELF: But you are quite wrong. It is true that the Bolshevists have sought to destroy beauty along with all other bourgeois diseases of the soul, and to that extent this doctrine is purely political. But it is also a brutal enunciation of much of the confused thought at the back of the Free Verse movement. It is more than that, indeed: it is, in my view, the logical conclusion of that theory, and, in spite of its superficial absurdities, it has a core of hard sense.

D.: Before you continue I should like to know whether you have the book in the hotel? Before I express a view on the theory I should like to see some example of the practice.

MYSELF: Yes, as a matter of fact, I have been reading it in bed. I'll go in and fetch it now. And won't you two go over to the other side of the terrace and order lunch, not forgetting three Vermouths mixed?

When I came back from my room I found R. and Delarue tasting their Vermouth and regarding the vast reaches of loveliness with a modified detestation. The sun of the early afternoon lay on the lake like patches of gold ink on heavy blue blotting-paper. From time to time a passing cloud scribbled a white blot that was rapidly absorbed into the blue. The nearer mountains bent their brown heads sleepily over their folded green arms, while behind them Mont Blanc poured up into space with not a breath of wind to disturb its

48

straight, white flame. Except for the clatter of plates, and the voices of the few people at lunch, the world was quiet. From far off cow-bells were sprinkling the hot air with their cool note, and a steamer screamed suddenly like a sea-bird round an elbow of the lake.

It seemed to me (and I imagine to the others) that here was the immutable answer to the Bolshevist theory, since, if the scene were the result of a purely mechanical arrangement, somebody would have to explain why this particular mechanical precipitation was so acutely (and generally) preferable to, say, the Mile End Road. I could see Delarue's uneasiness, and could almost feel him thinking that I was taking a most unfair advantage by permitting the silent advocacy of mountain, trees, and lake. But, for all that, when we returned to our chairs at the other end of the terrace, he did not sit with his back to the view, and there was a note of doubt in his voice when he asked me to read a poem from the Bolshevist book.

MYSELF: No, I don't think that I will. The poems, though admirably translated, add nothing to the theory. They are, frankly, dullish prose, but that may in part be due (though I don't believe it is) to the transference from Russian to English. I could find you a thousand poems in the modern American tradition wilder than these Rusian efforts, because the truth about the Russian seems to be that, while in practical affairs he is never as good as his theory, in art he is never as bad.

I had much rather take a few selections at random from serious contemporary Anglo-Saxon performers in this mode, and ask of them whether they are poetry, and if so why they are better than, and in what different from, what I have been accustomed to salute by that name.

D.: But before you start reading (and you will be good enough to read fairly) I should like to say that there is much sound sense in the Bolshevist theory vitiated only by political hydrophobia. It is radiantly true that the poet must use words as though they were spoken for the first time. He must strip them of the accumulated rubbish of centuries of half-meaning, and he must thrust them out of himself. They must stand like the units in a forlorn hope, waiting for action, each flushed with the terror and the glory of the unknown, stripped of the past, and touched with the twilight of the ineluctable future. Thus and thus only —

R.: I agree entirely, Delaruc; but what becomes of prose? Isn't prose, in fact, a consolidation of the base from which poetry sets out on its hazardous missions? Isn't poetry indeed the spirit set free for adventure into the unknown? Isn't that exactly the difference between the two — prose, rich in what it has, but poetry adorned with the unattainable?

D.: You are deserting me for the sentimentalists, R. That is not you, but the Château Neuf du Pape speaking to the debauching flute-music of that bewildering snow. I repeat in spite of all these insidious traps that there is no essential difference between the two, though I will admit that for the purpose of convenience we can speak of them separately as you can speak separately of right and wrong, well knowing that no such difference is in fact logically defensible. And I repeat that the Bolshevists are right in maintaining that the first step in art is to recognise the sovereignty of the material. Thereafter is the sphere of the artist, in the denial of which rests the Bolshevist error, as is demonstrable thus: I will give two men twenty words to fit into a poem, and one will make it into sing-song, the second into verse.

MYSELF: And how will you distinguish?

D.: By the courage in the words themselves. If they shoulder time away, if they create their own image-shadows, if they combine into a declaration against death, that will be a poem. But if they are easy, if they drift into time, if they have the facile, worn loveliness of rhyme, metre, and cadence, they will assert instead of refuting death — and that will be poetry as Wolfe understands (and indeed writes) it.

MYSELF: Let us, then, take a few examples chosen at random from the books that I had with me and which I found lying by the side of the Bolshevist book. I take Sacheverell Sitwell's new book first. I know that, though he is from time to time suspected of reaction, you admit him into your company. We will not take the Flower-Poems because these are poetry as I understand it — the sound, the exquisitely baffling image, the overtaking of time by beauty. Let us rather address ourselves to "Doctor Donne and Gargantua." Take, for example:

Pompey is an arrogant high hollow fateful rider
In noisy triumph to the trumpet's mouth,
Doomed to a clown's death, laughing into old age,
Never pricked by Brutus in the statue's shade.
But Cæsar and Pompey were dead pawns to me,
Moving down fields for ever fallow, never bearing,
And I cared not which killed the other,
Snatching his mock-life of me;
While Donne and Gargantua, each in his sphere,
Walks without me and has the populace to work upon,
Each can win, each can lose, each can break his paper
    life,
Tugging at that kite through the thick and fiery winds,
Foul breath of crowds, battle paintings, whispered
    words of fate,
Till the string break.
When their souls survive but must forage for them-
    selves,
For I cannot care for something that can never die.

It is, of course, not fair to criticise, or attempt to appreciate, the meaning of that apart from the context.

I do not therefore ask for an exegesis. But I do ask, is that poetry and, if so, why?

R.: A man must be tone-deaf if he can't find the authentic note in

arrogant high hollow fateful rider.

There, with accumulating vision, life stamps in empty braggadocio into the tragi-comedy of its circus-ring, death. The images are clear, resolute, and, above all, lonely. It has that element — the last seal of verse — loneliness.

D.: But again I should differ from you, R. For me, too, it is poetry, but the poetry is in the recognition of the "crowd's foul breath." The poetasters breathe and become a part of it, but the poet disinfects it for ever by setting it free in verse.

MYSELF: But after all, Delarue, that is the affair of a Sanitary Inspector or a Medical Officer of Health rather than of verse. Poetry is not a sort of immortal patchouli. To me — for whom Sacheverell Sitwell is a poet — I find no poetry here, except in the phrase R. has repeated. This seems emphatically prose in that it expresses, without the savage economies and the consequent spiritual echoes, certain aspects of life. But perhaps a better example even is afforded by "Marianna" from *Streets in the Moon,* that remarkable book by Archibald Macleish. This is a peculiarly good choice for our purpose, because it is a deliberate restatement of Tennyson's " Marianna in the Moated Grange."

> *He does not come —*
> *He cometh not, she said.*
>
> *He does not come —*
> *The strong sweet*
> *Probable hands,*
> *The expected feet,*
> *The arms have become*
> *Coffee at eight,*
> *Lunch at one,*
> *And the long wait*
> *From people for tea*
> *To people for dinner,*
> *From people for dinner*
> *Till sleep at three —*
>
> *Her bed jars*
> *To the passing cars.*
> *The air*
> *Fingers her hair.*
>
> *He does not come —*
> *He cometh not, she said.*
> *She said, My life is dreary —*

She yawns and extinguishes the light beside her bed.

54

And, perhaps you would urge, extinguishes Tennyson at the same time. But will you explain to me why the uprush into passion of

> *The strong sweet*
> *Probable hands,*
> *The expected feet*

must descend to coffee, lunch, dinner, and tea? Can a moated grange not be as beautiful as a chafing-dish? Must verse abjure the lighted torch for trouble with the municipal electric supply? In a word, have we come to believe that though one thing is as good as another, on the whole beautiful things are worse?

R.: Both Tennyson and Macleish have written real poems, but they are separated by about 100 years. If a moated grange has an actual and not a sentimental meaning, it is admissible just as a hot-water bottle, if seriously approached, may have lasting significance. Macleish has written a poem of real passion, because he has transfixed the diurnal futilities in a permanent sob. And I tell you, Delarue, that just that effect could in no circumstances have been produced by prose.

D.: Oh, I will call it poetry, if you like, because, like you, I respond to it emotionally, but I should have responded in exactly the same way if it had been spoken in a drawing-room.

MYSELF: Which is exactly what Matthew Arnold (I think) said of Wordsworth's

Will no one tell me what she sings?

Anybody listening to a young lady trying over a ballad, he suggested, might well have breathed that majestic cadence to his neighbour.

D.: Wordsworth says nothing to me, and Matthew Arnold classified himself when he described art as imitation. It is, of course, the one thing that true art does not do. The true artist and the true poem stand absolutely by themselves, independent both of life and their Creator.

MYSELF: That observation brings us back to the first possible criterion of verse that emerged in our conversation. A poem, you maintain, to be a poem must be different from all the work that has preceded it. That is in itself a platitude, but it becomes more if you add that a new poet must always make a new form. We could then affirm that any contemporary writer who composed a sonnet was courting certain failure. It would follow that when Ezra Pound wrote " Go from me now " his success was limited and, indeed, spoiled by the sonnet-form.

R.: I entirely agree. The time must come when any given form chokes itself. In spite of Austin Dobson, it can be declared, as axiomatic, that the old French forms are entirely incompatible with modern creative effort. The skeleton haunts you from the outset, and,

56

whatever flesh you impose upon those gaunt bones, they continue to show their osseous outline. I am not sure that the sonnet may not by this time have joined the derelict company of the rondeau, the ballade, and the villanelle. At any rate, it is certain that true poetry does adapt itself to some external movement in the time in which it is written. It remains, and must remain, the maximum of effort in the smallest possible compass. It will always be divine shorthand, but the system of notation adopted must vary from age to age.

MYSELF: Then in spite of Delarue we have begun to reach a differentiation between prose and verse, and the beginnings of a theory of the craft. Poetry is fundamentally concentration and economy. It would almost seem that there was a half-truth in the Bolshevist guess that you could distinguish between the two modes on an arithmetical basis. A half-truth only, because " The Ring and the Book " is a great deal longer and less economical than, say, " Urn-Burial." But the criterion on this showing will not be the number of words used, but the amount expressed by them.

D.: I confess that I am not convinced. I still hold that poetry differs no more from a novel than the novel from an essay. They are all three the use of the same raw material — words in a manner suited to the idiosyncrasy of the performer. The intrinsic difference is subjective rather than ultimately objective, and I will not for a moment admit that unconcentrated writing is more permissible in the novelist than the poet. The length is determined by the object to be expressed, and not by the method of expression. Let me take as an example of what I classify as prose — subdivision poetry — a very remarkable achievement of Max Jacob's:

" *Le général Japonais passe une revue des armées d'Europe. Son pantalon est si long qu'il fait le tire-bouchon vers les souliers. Au centre des armées est un évêque en surplis de dentelles devant une table de cuisine. L'évêque est gras, il a quelque poils au menton et de yeux pleins d'eau. Le Japonais anathématiserait bien l'évêque, mais il s'aperçoit qu'il l'a recontré dans le monde, il le regarde le salue et passe.*"

You cannot differentiate that from what is commonly called prose, and yet it achieves exactly what I seek in poetry. When I set out to write what is called a poem I seek to isolate some incident from the time-flux. Like Jacob, I want to preserve from the swirl the significant meeting of the Japanese general and the bishop. I concentrate, therefore, on an exact delineation. Having achieved it, I continue to pare away the traditional thought-deposits till it stands out clear, lonely, and absolute. I cannot hope to achieve absolute release, but the more the object is enfranchised the nearer I come to the complete poem, which, by virtue of the structure of the mind itself, nobody will ever write.

R.: But, Delarue, suppose that you had not rested content with that single, significant instant. Suppose you had wished to trace something of the life of the Japanese general, of the hesitations and spiritual disorders of the bishop. Suppose you had thought it necessary to describe the social world where the two had met, and suppose the result, instead of filling a dozen lines, had filled three hundred pages, would that still be a poem, or a novel? And if, in that event, a novel, in what does the distinction consist but in the fact that poetry illuminates by a series of lightning-flashes, prose by the level benevolences of the sun?

D.: You concede, then, that Jacob's exquisite fragment is poetry? If so, I —

Myself: I concede nothing of the sort, nor in his heart does R., Delarue. Let me tell you plainly that you can only maintain your position by destroying poetry altogether. If, for example, I say that walking is slow running I am merely using a silly figure of speech, but walking remains walking; running, running. But, if I go on to forbid all running on the ground that it is the same thing as walking, I have not abolished the distinction between the two. I have merely abolished running, an action explicable in a cripple, but not readily acceptable by a Greek athlete. In the same way you can go on calling poetry prose to your heart's content, as long as you don't write prose and call it poetry. And that, of course, is exactly what Jacob has done. I do not know French well enough to pronounce whether the meaningless little anecdote you have recited is good prose, but I know what poetry is well enough to know that it is not verse in French, or in any other civilised language under the sun. The plain fact is that it is the kernel of the possible novel, poem, or essay. But, having as yet no form, it proves nothing except the audacity or ignorance of the writer who publishes it as a finished product in any of these three divergent modes.

And as for your description of the way that you set about writing a poem, let me assure you that not only no poet, but no artist who ever lived, has created by theory, any more than a daffodil evolves in accordance with an Act of Parliament. The poet has an intense preoccupation with reality, and, as you rightly say, a reality in part independent of himself. But what he is seeking to do is not to liberate the object, but to set his own mind free, and his own heart at rest. So far he is not distinguishable from another artist. The distinction is in his medium. He does not use marble, or paints. He does not whisper the secret from the fiddle, nor the gold from the death of the sun. Nor, like the writer in prose, does he need to say everything. He has a short-cut to reality — by way of sound. He expresses himself in twelve lines, because some inexorable kinship between the ear and the prearranged sequence of words writes another thousand in the air and in the mind of the listener. He can be economical, because the harmonies he entreats are lavish, prodigal, unfathomable. He works, you see, supremely with thoughts as they reach the mind, and sounds as they reach the ear. When at last they perfectly fuse he has his poem.

You may reply that sound leaves you cold, that rhythm is an echo of bare and barbaric feet in a forest clearing, that rhyme is the chuckle of bones beaten at a savage dance. That may be true for you, and those who think with you. But it will not mean that poetry and prose are the same thing. It will mean only that, since one of the indispensable ingredients to this magic is wasted, poetry is dead, and it will mean that, if nobody can be found to renew the ancient enchantments, we had better admit that the golden bowl is broken, and the silver chord for ever loosed.

D.: If I were not amused by your rhetoric, my dear Wolfe, I should regard your outburst as not merely nonsense, but deliberately offensive nonsense. But I see how it is. You have been working off on us some speech you have been preparing for the plaudits of a young lady's tea-party. Spoken with a gesture, and learned by heart, I think that it would be effective in that environment. For my part, I will leave you to it and them, and will promenade myself among those less aggressive trees. If you have cooled down at dinner, I shall be ready to discuss on an amiable footing community singing, or any other topic of a kind which you may be expected to understand.

R.: My dear Humbert, that really is no way to conduct controversy. Delarue in his own way is a genuine poet, and it simply isn't decent to overwhelm him with what he quite justly calls prepared rhetoric. If you would only have given him time, he was on the way to admitting that economy was one of the integral elements of poetry.

MYSELF: Time, my dear R.! What he was claiming was eternity.

R.: Rubbish! He had reached the point, even in his description of his own methods of discovery to himself, that verse was a sort of enchanted pun, an eternal joke with one point to it — that is, the point of a spear. And then you pour abuse on the work of his friend Jacob. Naturally he fires up and goes off reflecting that the English remain in matters of art both violent and ignorant — and confirmed in his already considerable distaste for your own work.

MYSELF: That I will endeavour to support with such equanimity as heaven has lent me. But let us dismiss Delarue for the moment, and come back to a more equable discussion of our affair. We are agreed, as I understand it, that one indispensable element in verse is economy, or concentration. But that, you must also agree, will not take us very far. Would you be prepared to go one step further, and admit that that economy must be addressed not to the mind only, but the ear also? Would you, I mean, accept the contention that the approach of prose to the ear, as to the mind, can afford to be more lavish, and leisured — that verse is not only skating, but figure-skating?

R.: You are trying, I see, to make me admit that not only is music necessary to verse, but music of a particular, even traditional, kind. I do not know how I can accept that, at any rate as you advance it. It would be foolish to deny that in some of the world's greatest poetry the ear is simultaneously satisfied with the mind, and that the appeal of art in that case may be supposed to address itself to one sense more than in the case of prose. I will go further and admit that in my own case when I write verse I am never indifferent to sound, though I believe that I have never subordinated clarity of ultimate expression to seduction of the ear. But what does that mean? It means only, I think, that the mind has its rhythms, as the planets have their ascensions. But each mind, like each planet, must be true to its own weight, and you cannot have the negligible earth imitating the immense paces of Jupiter.

If you were prepared to agree that there were two rhythms — one for verse and one for prose — then I believe on that point, too, we might reach agreement. We should say that verse is the most economical expression consistent with lucidity, and adapted to its own rhythm, which will change not merely from generation to generation, but from poet to poet.

MYSELF: I am not sure that you go far enough. You say that prose and verse have each their own rhythm, but I do not find that you distinguish. Let us abandon for a moment the traditional forms and tests, and let us apply ourselves to a poem by T. S. Eliot, which I should heartily agree with you is a poem. I mean " The Hollow Men," and I quote (from memory — and I hope correctly!) the second stanza:

> *Eyes I dare not meet in dreams*
> *In death's dream kingdom,*
> *These do not appear:*
> *There, the eyes are*
> *Sunlight in a broken column;*
> *There, is a tree swinging*
> *And voices are*
> *In the wind's singing,*
> *More distant and more solemn*
> *Than a fading star.*
> *Let me be no nearer*
> *In death's dream kingdom.*
> *Let me also wear*
> *Such deliberate disguises —*
> *Rat's coat, crowskin, crossed staves —*
> *In a field*
> *Behaving as the wind behaves.*
> *No nearer —*
> *Not that final meeting*
> *In the twilight kingdom.*

Now by our first test this is indubitably verse, since it drops one beam into a huge darkness. You see the small light betrayed even as it falls by mortality, and all about and beyond sway the dark and dangerous edges of the unknown. That is true and beautiful economy. And now the rhythm — nobody will dispute its presence, even to the existence, accidental or designed, of rhyme. Yes, I will admit not only that there is cadence, but that what is said here is said in verse, because it could not have been said exactly so in prose. But if I admit this for the rest of the poem, how am I to apply the same test to the two last verses:

> *Between the desire*
> *And the spasm,*
> *Between the potency*
> *And the existence,*
> *Between the essence*
> *And the descent,*
> *Falls the shadow —*
> > *For Thine is the Kingdom.*

> *For Thine is,*
> *Life is:*
> *For Thine is the . . .*
> *This is the way the world ends,*
> *This is the way the world ends,*
> *This is the way the world ends —*
> *Not with a bang, but a whimper.*

I think I know why Eliot wrote these last lines just so. They represent disintegration. They represent tangled, broken whispers from the illimitable background of human experience, fused, muddled, misunderstood, and in decay. But, if I eagerly maintain that the first stanza is verse, and good verse, I should still feel that here was a deliberate introduction of prose to indicate that, when all fails and founders, verse fails and founders with the rest.

R.: The end of the poem seems to me to be as indubitably poetry as the rest. It is as sovereign as the line

But what may quiet us in an end so noble.

It is merely a question of acclimatising the ear. There is a sound-pattern as definite, though naturally more delicate than that in a sonnet.

MYSELF: But, if you grant me the pattern, tell me how, otherwise than by concentrated arrangement, does it differ from a prose-pattern.

R.: If it will help you, I will grant you that, but I do not see what difference it makes.

MYSELF: But it makes all the difference in the world. We shall now be able to see why some of the absurdities of free verse, possibly as prose, are, in fact, absurd as verse. We shall say to some of Delarue's friends, for example, "What you write is not prose, because it is meaningless. But that is carrying economy a little far. Verse expresses the most possible in the least space, not

66

the least possible." Moreover, we shall be able to say to them that they must realise that they have to direct themselves to the ear as well as to the mind. They have only to carry their doctrine one step further to agree with Bolshevism, that, action being better than art, all verse should be action. But if in pursuit of this theory they choose to precipitate themselves from a second-floor window, neither their flight through the air nor any groans they may utter during the incident will be verse. In the last resort, like all other forms of art, verse imposes the limits (and the magic) of its material, which are thought and sound.

R.: I daresay that I should not too actively dissent from all this. But, further, I should ask myself of the wildest verse whether it may not be moulding a rhythm which, through some form of deafness, I cannot overhear. If I had been a contemporary of Browning's, I might very well have joined with all those who tried to laugh him out of court. And how do I know that some of the apparently ridiculous American free-verse writers are not, as it were, singing just round the corner?

MYSELF: Let us have a little courage. There is no form of artistic blackmail more insidious than that which makes us afraid of denouncing creative follies for fear of being adjudged as blind to new talent. Obviously, again and again in literary history an innovator has been wrongly mocked, but that only makes it the more important that we should endeavour to detect and to brand the pseudo-innovation. And I think it will be true to say that the true innovator is never a century ahead of his generation, but generally about ten years. When, therefore, we are presented with inchoate noises like those offered for our amusement by the Dadaists, we can only say with certainty that these are so alien to the shape of the contemporary mind that they can mean nothing to their inventors either. Browning, for example, in his best work was easily intelligible during his lifetime, and indeed the difficulty of understanding him was not so much absolute as conditioned by the incredible facility with which Tennyson could be apprehended.

We shall be quite safe, therefore, in asking of our poets that they shall concentrate thought and sound, and that, if they are to be great poets, they are to use the combination with authority.

R.: I suppose you want me to ask what you mean by authority. But I know what you mean, because it is your habitual argument. You have in mind the distinction which Norman Douglas draws in " South Wind " between a magnificent locomotive-engine and a Greek sculpture of the great period. The first does not dominate the mind of the spectator, however much it may attract him. The second holds him by authority. That is true — even a truism. But it only means, if applied to verse, that a good poet's work is permanent, or as permanent as paper, ink, and the processes of the earth's age will allow.

MYSELF: It means more. It means that the magic poet of all times recreates his material, and in the moment of recreation astonishingly assimilates his expression to that of his predecessors and of those who follow him. Take at random half a dozen lines from the world's great poets at their greatest moments, and observe their fundamental kinship. Take Vergil's

> *I, decus, I, nostrum, melioribus utere fates.*

Take Chaucer's

> *The statue of Venus glorious for to see*
> *Was naked fleeting in the large sea.*

Take Marlowe's

> *Is it not passing great to be a king, Techelles,*
> *And ride in triumph through Persepolis?*

Take Cleopatra's cry:

> *. . . lord of lords,*
> *O infinite virtue, comest thou smiling from*
> *The world's great snare uncaught?*

Take Donne's

> *I long to speak with some old lover's ghost*
> *Who died before the god of love was born.*

Take Andrew Marvell's

> *He nothing common did, or mean*
> *Upon that memorable scene,*
> *But with his keener eye*
> *The axe's edge did try.*
>
> *Nor called the gods with vulgar spite*
> *To vindicate his helpless right,*
> *But bowed his comely head*
> *Down, as upon a bed.*

Take Keats's

The voice I hear this passing night was heard
* In ancient days by emperor and clown;*
Perhaps the self-same song that found a path
* Through the sad heart of Ruth when, sick for home,*
She stood in tears amid the alien corn;
* The same that oft-times hath*
Charmed magic casements, opening on the foam
* Of perilous seas, in faery lands forlorn.*

Take Shelley's

> *My name is Ozymandias, king of kings.*
> *Look on my works, ye mighty, and despair.*

Take Goethe's

> *Über allen Gipfeln*
> *Ist Ruh*
> *In allen Wipfeln*

Spürest du
Kaum einen Hauch.
Die Vöglein schweigen im Walde.
Warte nur; balde
Ruhest du auch.

Take Victor Hugo's

Je puis dire maintenant aux rapides années,
Passez, passez toujours, je n'ai plus à vieillir.
Allez-vous en avec vos fleurs toutes fanées,
J'ai dans mon âme une fleur que nul ne peut cueillir.

Votre aile en le heurtant ne fera rien répandre
Du vase, ou je m'abreuve et que j'ai bien rempli.
Mon âme a plus de feu que vous n'avez de cendre;
Mon cœur a plus d'amour que vous n'avez d'oubli.

These are all toys so worn that I am almost ashamed to quote them. But, varying from age to age, from language to language, from form to form, they have fundamentally the same calm accent of finality. They do not ask, they do not hint, they do not hesitate. They demand, and they compel. It is not a question only of subject-matter; it is not only the vastness of the conception. It is that here sound and thought, because they have been born again, have found the life everlasting. And taken together they prove that great verse, like all great art, is not the product of chemical, but of organic combination.

As a man who writes to illustrate a theory becomes himself an illustration of the fact that the letter kills, at the great moment the poet follows no theory: he is the theory.

R.: The trouble about all discussion of verse is that you end by metaphors, and by personal preferences. You say that all these lines have the same calm accent. But may that not be because we hear them all across the years, and is it not certain that there are a hundred contemporary lines that will in the passage of time acquire that quality? If it is only their calmness that enraptures you, then you are doing no more than if you said that all old and great pictures had a uniform quality of colour — due in its softness and richness, not to the painter, but to Time. You would do better to extract the quality they have in common. Is it that all these give

What oft was thought, but ne'er so well exprest,

or are they expressing universal truths for the first time? I will answer my own question, and my answer will be that there is nothing in the world that has not a genuine significance. The poet elicits that significance, and relates it to something beyond itself and beyond his own mind.

There are pine-woods below our feet, and the evening is coming upon them and the lake. The beauty of day is yielding to the darker charm of night. So

Life passes from one beauty to another. But beyond the mountains is another world, and there, too, changes that we cannot see, but at which we faintly guess, are advancing in their inevitable order. And when Goethe spoke of peace on the mountains — clear, stainless peace — and the silence of the wood-birds, when he saw in that a promise of peace for the restless heart, he related that transient significance of loveliness to the untransient peace that neither he nor any of us can know.

If that analysis be true, then it can, *mutatis mutandis,* be applied to all the other lines you have quoted, and we may find in that, perhaps, part of the explanation for which we are seeking.

MYSELF: Indeed, we may, and we shall be entitled to, go further and say that it is such significance expressed exactly and only by the medium of which we have spoken. All great art isolates and relates that significance, but each by its own path. It is for that reason that those of us who care for verse fight furiously to prevent the boundaries from being obscured. We do not pretend that other arts have not an equal value, but we insist that it is different. We will not talk of architecture in terms of a novel, or painting of music. We believe that each has its own irreplaceable contribution.

It may be that some new art may arise — like that of the cinema — which will appeal to three senses at once; or that of a future one that appeals to five. But these must not be allowed to blur the purity of the arts that exist. And of those that exist verse is always in the greatest danger of invasion, because part of its material is the same as that of prose. We must, therefore, have no truce with the invader, or, if the invasion is permitted, we must agree that poetry, as Sophocles, Villon, Shakespeare, and Beaudelaire knew it, is over. And a new art has taken its place.

R.: Well, then, you conclude that verse is the expression with authority of what is significant in life by means of the fusion of thought and sound. I am not sure, do you know, that that is much more than to say that poetry is, in short, poetry.

MYSELF: Well, at least, it is better than saying that it is prose. But we can perhaps test and explore our formula a little further if we apply it to one or two established contemporary reputations, and see how they and the standard emerge. We could do worse, I think, than start with Thomas Hardy, who has for some time past been conceded a place as a fixed star almost beyond criticism. Nor, at first sight, is that surprising, if we look at his verse from the point of view of the formula. As to Hardy's authority there can be no question. We speak of a " Hardy country " in the map of England: there is equally one in the map of the mind — a bleak, harsh country of black moorland against a dull and windy sky, a (to me) wholly distasteful country, and yet one from which, in opening his books, I can no more escape than I can dismiss Manchester when

74

emerging from the gloomy public slaughter-house which has been roughly adapted by the railway company to serve for a station. Hardy imposes his country, because it has been reborn out of his blood and bone, and he is as sure of it as if it were his walking-stick. So much for authority. As to significance, here again there can be no question. Hardy has examined life and found it wanting, but wanting rather as an idiot is wanting, or as a toy designed by a malicious zany, signifying not nothing, but something with a faintly confused and malevolent purpose — like a very fat man in pumps aimlessly trampling a rose into the mud, and spattering his shoes and socks in the process. Oh, there is significance and related significance — for his babbling and aimless laughter spreads out beyond the world. You can conceive its tinny echo disturbing Lethe. There remains then the form, and it is here where my personal doubt of Hardy as a poet creeps in. It is not open to dispute that he uses the traditional forms of verse, and to that extent we might pass him on that score without further argument. But, of course, we should be wrong. As you have rightly said, the rhythm must, like that of a planet, be true to its weight. As long as it is a true rhythm, a poet may either write like Austin Dobson or like the prophet Isaiah; all that we ask is that Isaiah shall not use the rondeau nor Dobson cry like the satyr to his fellow. There is no question that Hardy's rhythm is as significant as his subject-matter, and that it is profoundly his own. But in my view, except in a very few instances, it is not the rhythm of verse, but of prose. I do not say that because it is a clumsy and deliberately harsh rhythm; that is sometimes true of Browning's best verse. Nor because it is insensitive — that is in part the heritage of the Anglo-Saxon words, which Hardy prefers. But I say it because it is slow, gradual rhythm that to me has exactly the same cumulative effect as a chapter-ending in *Tess* or *The Return of the Native*. It is not that he cannot use sound, but it is that sound does not for him rank side by side with significance as of first-rate importance. He hammers, but he does not melt, his words. They are just words, justly placed, but they speak. In a word, Hardy does everything except sing, and, if that is true, he is everything but a poet; because by our norm the poet will have to give equal weight to all his materials, and poetry will be the fusion of all of them. It seems to me definitely that there is no twilight of music in his poetry, beguiling the mind and suggesting what is true because it is impossible of apprehension.

R.: If that conclusion flows from the application of our standard, then, in my view, the standard is wrong. But I believe it is your application and not the standard which is at fault. Sometimes, as Hardy himself says, if you stand on a moor on a clear night of stars, you have suddenly the sensation of the earth itself moving, an immense wheel through space. There is, I am sure, that impulse in some music, and for me it is in Hardy's verse. You cannot easily feel it: if you are dull or impatient, you may miss it altogether. But if you will possess yourself with loneliness, you will swing with his movement through space. You will have not the music of the spheres, but the lonely, humbler, but untroubled movement of earth itself. That is why, for me, Hardy is a great poet, and why our standard is justified by application to him.

But let us take another reputation, upon which we are not likely to differ — that of W. B. Yeats. We shall find in him in varying degrees obedience to all the tests. If we invert the order we need not delay ourselves in the control of sound. No English poet moves more securely in the climate of overtones. So audible are the unspoken echoes that the written word has something ghostly in it, as though it were aware that its substance was always beyond the veil. As to significance, if his words have the air of shadows it is because life for him is like shadows of the clouds blowing over a sunny field. But with always a touch of the cold in the last shadow. He writes of legendary figures not because they are real, but because we are unreal, or half unreal. And, as to authority, he admits us to the misery of the knight " alone and palely loitering," so that we in turn are held by that immortal disenchantment.

MYSELF: That is true, but I would add that Yeats fails of ultimate greatness, because both the significance and authority are in the end those of the dream. That quiet, not of the earth, those faint and motionless margins, fail for me of immortality because they claim it. Yeats writes like a changeling, and therefore he does not know that the tragedy of mortality is not that we have lost our fairylands, but that there are no fairylands to lose.

Let us take Rudyard Kipling as our last reputation, and we had better hurry. They are lighting the great lamps on the terrace, and I think their light will bring our French moth flitting back to risk his wings again, a spectacle which I had rather avoid. We shall not, I think, deny Kipling's authority. You may resent, but you cannot resist, his domination. He says to one emotion " go," and it goes; to a prejudice " come," and it comes. We are in the presence of an art that imposes itself. I leave " significance " for the moment and pass to sound-control. Here there are, of course, two Kiplings — the Kipling who plays the saxophone because he actually prefers it to the fiddle, and the Kipling who plays the fiddle because something greater than himself has taken the saxophone away from him — generally without the poet's knowledge. In the first mood he makes the clatter to which his strong, silent men are accustomed to move by natural contrast; in the other he has surrendered himself and his heroes to the still, small voice that will none of them or of jazz. It is an astonished oboe playing after the Pan-pipes of a merry-go-round at a fair have suddenly ceased; it is a flute played in the middle of the election meeting for the American Presidency. He has, therefore, authority, and at rare intervals those elusive lovelinesses of rhythm. What then, of significance? When he has something significant to say, then, by some divine rightness, the oboe or the flute are at his command. To the wilderness of political propaganda, or imperial spite, the jazz rhythms flock, and roar and rattle like macaws. But when the Kipling of the great short stories, of *Kim,* and *The Jungle Books* is suddenly brought face to face with the brevity of life, with youth that is gallant and doomed, with childhood prevented by Fate — music, authority, and significance flash together, and he is in those brief instants a poet.

R.: And if the test applies so to Hardy, Yeats, and Kipling, to whom of our immediate contemporaries dare we apply it — T. S. Eliot, Edith Sitwell, D. H. Lawrence, Harold Monro, James Stephens, Edmund Blunden, or Robert Graves? Can we ask how any of them would emerge? Would it, perhaps, be said of all of them that, whatever other merit they have, they have not authority? And shall we be driven in consequence, and with profound reluctance, to deny to them all the appellation of "major poet," which, for example, Arnold Bennett applied to Robert Graves?

MYSELF: No, I do not think so. Authority is in a sense a retrospective quality. A young poet — even a young poet of genius — cannot give that impression with his earliest work. It is a little like the colour of the Old Masters of which we spoke earlier. It is, in part, the gift of Time. Or it is like reading an earlier Conrad, for example, *The Secret Agent*. You read through, waiting for something miraculous to happen, and then suddenly, almost at the last page, a bell rings. You go back to the beginning and you can hear the premonitory whisper that escaped you at first reading. So it may be with some of those that you mention. So it seems to me to be emphatically both with Brooke and Flecker. They had significance which might have deepened; they had the singing-note. They have the authority of the lover on the Greek vase. If they had lived, they might have had the authority of Keats.

R.: But Keats was younger than either of them when he died.

MYSELF: Who knows what Keats would have written if he had lived? Shelley and Keats — the Dioscuri — who wheel together in that abundant sky: who knows what eternal authority was quenched by the invidious dark?

DELARUE: The invidious dark — is that where your argument has ended?

MYSELF: Perhaps, but at least they have lit the lamps of earth on the terrace. Let me, by way of apology, offer you dinner and a willing ear, in the little light that they afford.

English Bards and French Reviewers

"The curious thing about it all is that M. André Maurois, unlike so many of his compatriots, actually likes the English. You might have imagined, therefore —" But perhaps I had better begin at the beginning of the conversation in an imaginary room in the Cour de St. Pierre at Geneva.

And first, since the room is imaginary, let us imagine it. It will be on the lower side of the square, facing the beech that grows out of the sloping cobbles, and the Mädchenhaus in the Place de la Taconnerie. It will, of course, be irrigated by the little water-clear notes of the Cathedral chimes, set by a campanologist in love with a musical-box. Yes, the two tall windows of the one side will be safely enfolded in that gentle square that even Calvin could not unmellow. But, if these windows are so enclosed, the two at the other end of the long, low room will open — well, not on eternity, but at least on a huge drop over peaked roofs to the lake and the Jura, like a herd of grazing elephants, wearing (since it is winter) white elephant-cloths on their huge flanks. Absolute silence, except for the quarterly bells; and candles in the sconces!

Myself: You think, then, that our English language is so unmanageable that it can only aspire to the severe forms of art, when strained off in the regular moulds of rhyme and rhythm? It is, as I understand you, a sort of iron-ore that must be melted out of the stone before it can be put to higher uses.

FIRST INTELLIGENT FRENCHMAN: No, I do not go so far as that. For to say of a foreign tongue that it is not capable of prose would be merely insolence. I venture the opinion, however, that your words are like one of your Bank Holiday crowds — very many, very gay, but rather indistinguishable, and stuck together. Very effective on the whole, but by themselves — will you forgive what might sound impertinent? — a little sheepish. They do not stand, easily and gracefully, in small and sculptural groups. They have force, more indeed than our French words, but far more than those they need the poet's parade orders.

MYSELF: Would you go so far as to deny "style" to all our English prose-writers? I pass over our Prayer-Book, and Sir Thomas Browne. I do not even cite Sterne, or Jane Austen. I give you moderns only — George Meredith, Joseph Conrad, and, above all, Bernard Shaw. We think that they compare not unfavourably with your Flaubert, Maupassant, and Marcel Proust.

F. I. F.: Your mention of Shaw in that gallery surprises me, and I would have to reflect a little before replying. But for the other two I have no doubts whatever. Style must flow out of the nature of the writing. It must not be added, like icing on a cake, or stone-icing on the iron-girders of a modern building. It is the sense of completeness achieved in each individual part. This does not mean that the disarrangement of a word would destroy the harmony, as would a slipped syllable in a rhythm, but it does mean that it should give the reader that impression. With Meredith and Conrad you could omit not only words, but pages, without producing any noticeable reaction. Meredith indeed is, in our view, pure or rather impure stucco. He falls short even of the baroque, because his is a heavy, and not a light-hearted, eccentricity. Conrad, on the other hand, has found the English language too tough for him, or so I judge. Those huge, undigested, and perhaps indigestible slabs of beauty! The effect is like Rodin, except that, whereas Rodin often leaves a part of his design unfinished of set purpose, Conrad leaves it all unfinished. Flaubert would have found much to admire in Conrad — in the way of raw material.

MYSELF: Dear me! You express yourself with some certainty! You will perhaps forgive me if I retort that your language owes its reputation to its actual poverty. It has, in its literary use, a certain affinity to the Japanese " Noh " poems. It is not its actual beauty, nor what it expresses, for both of these are, to us, very little. It is rather that the words, being so few, acquire a sort of repetition value. You cannot see the word for the shadows, nor hear its sound for the echoes. But, to leave this exchange of ranging shots, let us come to your Proust. He has, I believe, a high reputation in France?

F. I. F.: And in England!

MYSELF: The peculiar habit of the English is to believe that all good things come from abroad — in order to get away from the foreigners! You must not pay too much attention to our estimate of your literature. Why, there are actually those amongst us who profess an admiration of your Sur-réalistes!

F. I. F.: And my God! Why not?

MYSELF: Because in my view the imitation of the stammer of a rat decaying in a gutter is not art! But it is Proust with whom I am concerned. In what does he, for example, surpass Arnold Bennett?

F. I. F.: But precisely in the manner of "style." Mr. Bennett cannot, for example, stand still. He must move to be alive. It is a fault, even a grave fault. It is, in effect, the difference between a bird and an aeroplane. Proust has, naturally, the bird's quality of repose, or seeming repose. He does not need to agitate his wings to prove that he can fly. I do not blame Mr. Bennett. He has done almost all that the Teuton structure of the language will permit. The great, hulking words are such that, if they are not constantly hustled, they relapse into sulky heaps. Proust with the same material might have done no better. His good fortune was that, being

86

a Frenchman, his raw material was Mr. Bennett's finished article.

Myself: Do you suggest, then, that " style " is sufficient in itself? In an Olympic runner, for example, it is excellent to race with the action of the wind itself. The prize, however, is awarded to him who arrives first. There is something, is there not, to be said for having a goal!

F. I. F.: The stylist carries his goal about with him. He is always there. No struggle (at least none visible), no effort! Consider, for example, our Anatole France — not a very great writer as true greatness is measured. But set him beside your Wells! It is sculpture beside a cotton-mill. With France a single gesture crystallises a generation. With Wells it requires a generation to crystallise a gesture.

Myself: If you descend to epigram! But listen! You have chosen your two protagonists well. You admit of France, I think, that he has less substance than other stylists (the very few!) as great as himself, while we freely admit that Wells, who has infinite substance, splashes about, like an elephant engaged in the decoration of the Albert Hall. Yet I believe finally that Wells will outlast France. I will tell you why. Anatole fits with such delicate precision into the mind that ultimately he will not generate enough friction to be noticeable. But Wells will always have enough grit on the surface to prove an irritant. I can imagine a time when Anatole France will be a collector's piece. Wells, on the other hand, will continue to sprawl in anybody's sitting-room, and perhaps — who knows? — in the kitchen.

F. I. F.: I make you a present of the kitchen. With us it provides a standard rather for dishes than art. But its mere mention in such a context does, I think, throw a light on the profound gulf that separates our two nations in their approach to literature. To us it still seems that the English in this respect are at best brilliant amateurs, who on occasion have astounding luck. The English writer is not in the presence of a literary Code Napoléon relentlessly administered by the High Court of the Academy. As your Kipling says, he walks by himself and all places are alike to him — the kitchen, the salon, and the slopes of Parnassus. This licence is, in our view, in itself a fatal weakness. The Englishman is like a dancer, who sets about the Russian ballet without realising that there is a multitude of carefully studied steps and positions to be acquired, and that, further, great dancing consists in subordinating these steps to a new impetus, but never in neglecting them. It may happen — indeed it does happen — that immense talent produces first-rate results in spite of the absence of the necessary grounding. But it is certain, in our view, that with such a grounding a success even greater would be achieved. The Frenchman who desires to write has to submit to a discipline of extreme severity. The discipline defeats the vast majority. Of the rest a number become merely jugglers, producing their notes with the colourless certainty of a pianola. But the very few achieve a quite amazing force, because, the difficulties surmounted, they can never fall back into slackness or disorder. With a material comparatively limited they can evolve a bewildering series of patterns. But these patterns, as in great music, are always implicit in, and for ever revert to, the original motif. The great French writer ends by falling in love with his difficulties, and, in his highest moments, he translates the Aristotelian formula into romance by presenting the time and the place and the loved one altogether.

MYSELF: I think that what you have just said would perhaps be most satisfactorily tested by considering it in relation to verse. But I will, if I may, for a moment delay that exercise and remind you of our excursion to St. Cergue. You will remember how, on leaving Geneva, you observed that the town had the neat air of a story by de Maupassant. "It is perfectly complete," you said, " is composed without effort, has in the old buildings a hint of mortality, even of ruin, and presents itself, as a whole, without emphasis, and without a moral, as a purely objective circumstance. Looking at it, you do not realise what immense difficulties the grouping of the lake, with the Saleve on one side and the Jura on the other, presented. You forget that there

must be some slight reference to the distant, but dominating, glory of the White Mountain, and that, above
all, the whole must pass through the crucible of Calvin-
ism. Do you observe these difficulties? You do not. The
town appears to have grown haphazard, but I venture
to suggest that the laws dictating its growth were as
delicate and severe as those that regulate the leaf, bud,
and flower of the Alpine rose. In other words, as I
began by saying, a story by de Maupassant." You will
not forget that when we reached Nyon the autumn
sunshine, busy about the little Castle, had a disturb-
ingly lawless beauty. I pointed out that it did not seem
to be observing the mute " e," but was, as our Meredith
put it, " shouting with golden shouts " at our rather
lethargic senses. You did not agree, but you were —
confess it — a little shaken. Then we reached St. Cergue
(m. 1,020) by the little train, and walked, in growing
doubt on your side and ecstasy on mine, up the steep
paths through the pine-woods half-way to the Dôle.
As you know, I have no skill with prose, and, if my
description of what we saw is inadequate, you must
be fair and impute the failure to me rather than to the
English language. But the thing is worth attempting
because it provides, in my view, an answer to your
claim for Geneva and de Maupassant. We reached the
top of a hill about five hundred feet below the Dôle,
and about that height above St. Cergue. It was perfectly
still, except for the incessant stir of innumerable cicadas
winding their watches. The sky was cloudless, and the

sun walked between the pines, like a conqueror in procession between tall, green flag-staffs of triumph. Yes, that was already something to challenge your theory, but there was more. Not a leaf had fallen from the trees, and, except for the dark needles of the pine, not a leaf was green. For mile after mile the forests glowed like a spilt sunset that glittered about our feet hour after hour. Or, to take another picture, in some of the woods the dark pines slid towards us, like green galleons, over a tossing spray of coloured sea. And you will remember that a lark, out of his season and place, shot up, trailing the whole of that loveliness carelessly in a shining wake of song. "That," I observed, "is English literature." You had, I believe, some doubt at that moment as to the ultimate value of de Maupassant.

F. I. F.: I am no judge of your prose, and I cannot, therefore, say whether your effort is good or bad, though I admit that your description does in a measure recall the emotions of that moment. But your performance, however remarkable, does with extraordinary aptness illustrate my contention. I give you, as I believe, a reasonably logical explanation of the difference between the two literatures. Upon that explanation I base the claim that the best French professional achieves a higher solution than the best English amateur, and how do you retort? By breaking all the rules of controversy, and by substituting for logic a barefaced *argumentum ad,* not *hominem,* but, I would say, *mulierem.*

You appeal to the woman in me, and, having, you hope, dazed my emotions, you ask for the verdict. Well, I am not taken in by your three-card trick. I have, as you say in your slang, "spotted the lady" — and I remind you that logic is an affair for men. I will, therefore, merely say that an autumn sunset at St. Cergue proves nothing whatever, except perhaps a rather charming susceptibility in yourself. The test would be to find a rendering of that event, say, both by the lamented Anatole and your Conrad. France would have given it all in a couple of sentences — decisive, clear, and apparently trifling. And certainly there would have been a touch of ironic order in his stroke. He would not have left Nature to her rather chaotic self, but would have superimposed on her too expensive beauty the critical loveliness of the perfect human mind. Conrad, on the other hand, I conceive, might have written fifty pages as long, and as wild, as the affair itself. It would have fallen almost as inconsequently into his novel as it fell into our lives — a mass of undigested and unrelated beauty. Now, at the bottom of our French practice there is a philosophic theory, almost paradoxically a protest against realism. It is the assertion that man is the maker, and in our most absolute objectivity we retain the most absolute control. And, since man has so short a time here, the great French writers aim at the severest possible compression. You remember, for example, how Anatole summed up a century of scepticism in the last sentence of the first story of *L'Etui de Nacre*: " *Jésus de Nazareth! je ne me rappele pas.*"

MYSELF: I am afraid that we are becoming rather discursive, and drifting away from the original point of our conversation, which was the curious attitude of mental superiority that your best people adopt to our poets. I will come back to that in a moment. Just now I am distracted by your allusion to Anatole France's story of Pontius Pilate. It put me in mind at once of another sceptical account of the Nazarene. I have in mind George Moore's *The Brook Kerith*. I will not conceal from you that I am almost blinded with admiration for that wonderful book, and that I may, therefore, be speaking of it a little uncritically. But I choose it because George Moore has taken four hundred and seventy-one pages to express what you claim that your Anatole France polished off in a sentence. You might, perhaps, urge before I say more on this point that a fairer comparison would be with Renan's *Vie de Jésus*. But I hardly think so. For we are here in the climate of the deliberately fictitious, or, as you would say, in a situation where " in our most absolute objectivity we retain the most absolute control." I maintain, therefore, the juxtaposition of Moore and France. Now, from your point of view, George Moore is particularly interesting. His early literary years were spent in France. He soaked himself in French literature and art. He prefaced *The Confessions of a Young Man* with a dedication to

Jacques Blanche in what he may quite possibly have believed to have been French prose. And I daresay that he conceives himself always to have been governed by French standards. Well, *The Book Kerith* is an account of the life of Christ. You probably know Moore's story? No! The first and larger part is presented through the eyes of Joseph of Arimathea, who might have been, in Moore's version, the young man who turned away "because he had many possessions." Joseph is the type of all those many thousands after him, who have loved Jesus with a love passing that of woman, but could not find it in themselves to give up all and follow him. Up to the Crucifixion the story is told with a radiant simplicity both of language and action, which still contrives to net the elusive perfume of that incredibly moving Personality. There was nothing like it in English, till Bernard Shaw invented his St. Joan, and that conception falls as far short of George Moore's as did the saint of the Nazarene. The first part of the story follows the Gospels fairly closely, though naturally the presentation is entirely humanised through the medium of the gentle, lovable, and adoring Joseph. After the Crucifixion the story is, of course, George Moore's own. For Christ does not die on the Cross, but is lifted down by Joseph and nursed back to something like health. Finally he is taken secretly out of Jerusalem by Joseph and restored, as their shepherd, to the Essenes, a severe Jewish order, with whom, according to Moore, Jesus had served in his youth. And here is the culmination of the story, and the point at which the comparison with France becomes so stinging. Jesus finds that his flock has been almost destroyed by bad shepherding, thieves, and the want of a ram. The Beloved Shepherd searches through all the unfriendly hills for His ram, and finally comes upon one, when He Himself is almost at the last gasp of exhaustion. The ram is a newly born one of a great breed, but is given to Him because it is like to die. Jesus staggers back the long, long way across the hills, bearing the baby ram in His bosom. It lives, and the herd is restored. I set that Figure against the slick perfection of Anatole France's Pontius. With France there is the metallic click of absolute, if exquisite, negation. With George Moore's, the world's passionate belief in that adored Figure is given a heartbreaking, but none the less completely positive, twist. Here is Jesus, who, they believed, saved the flocks of the world, saving a little flock of sheep on the hills of Palestine. I do not believe that anybody could read George Moore's account without feeling his heart turn over. I am not sure that in reading Anatole France's epigram even the mind turns over. I claim the returning Shepherd for English literature. I give you the Roman procurator in his litter at the baths.

F. I. F.: It would have been fairer, on what you say, to have compared Moore with Renan. But I am not sufficiently familiar with Moore to continue the argument with him as an illustration. We had better, I think, go on to poetry. But before that we will dine; and after dinner Jocquelin is coming in. You know that he has already a considerable reputation as in the legitimate succession to the Parnassians. I find you a more obdurate antagonist than I had anticipated, and I shall not be sorry to have Jocquelin's assistance.

MYSELF: Dinner by all means; but don't pretend that you think that I have had the better of the argument. For you know that in your mind you are convinced that we have each of us proved conclusively, not that either is right or wrong, but that the gulf between the English and French conceptions is not to be bridged.

You will now be good enough to permit me to imagine the dinner as you have permitted me to imagine the room and the conversation. The table will be set for two at the window looking over the roofs to the lake and the Jura. The lake will be all strung with arc-lamps, shining like Chinese lanterns at a ball, and above the Jura, looking like stage mountains, inaccessible because they aren't there, the greater Chinese lantern of a yellow moon will slowly suspend itself from the invisible branches of heaven. There will be, of course, amusing things to eat, as, for example, that queer blue trout-fish *féras* from the lake, and something truffled to follow. And we shall drink, I think, Mont d'Or, that Swiss wine put up in hock bottles, with a faint sub-acid hint of bubbles — not by any means a good wine, but the Swiss grapes can never quite shake themselves free of the snow. There is a certain self-protective asperity. Presently we shall be smoking the perfectly good "Gold Flake" cigarettes that Messrs. Wills surprisingly manufacture in Switzerland, and there will be a knock at the door, and M. Jocquelin will enter, and with him French poetry.

F. I. F.: Ah, Jocquelin! You have met, I think, Mr. Humbert Wolfe! He has a certain interest in literature, having actually, so they inform me, attempted something on his own account. His interest for us, however, is that he has, it seems to me, a more than average knowledge of his country's literature, and, if I may say so without offence, rather more knowledge of ours than is common with the English. In these circumstances, his views on the comparative importance of the two have a certain interest. We have, for the last two hours or so, been ranging among the prosaists. We have had comparisons of Bennett and Proust, Anatole France and George Moore, which have, I'm afraid, taken us very little further. I still maintain that it is a contest between professionals and amateurs, and he, I think, would say that to be a professional is in itself a confession of failure. We are agreed, however, that we shall bring the conversation to an issue if we bring poetry into the field. It is in this that I particularly welcome your assistance, because our friend, though he has in no way convinced me, maintains his position stoutly enough. And, by the way, I think it will be best if we continue the conversation each in his own language. For none of us is, I think, sufficiently adept at the foreign tongue to be convincing.

M. Jocquelin: I suppose that what has been in discussion is the almost threadbare quarrel that may be called, for the sake of brevity, the Racine-Shakespeare problem. Shakespeare, as we know, has only been generally recognised in France in the last fifty years, and Racine, as I understand, is not yet recognised at all in Great Britain. Now this, in my view, crystallises the whole question. Shakespeare has the whole of British opinion as solidly behind him as Racine the French, and yet we have this bewildering diversity of view between the two nations. This would produce a feeling of despair as to the validity of any literary reputation, if we did not find that the French and English were equally prepared to salute neutral writers, as, for example, Vergil and Sophocles. We are, therefore, compelled to consider how the difference of opinion arises, what its justification is, and which, if either, of the nations is to blame. And I observe this: In your latest school of thought, that represented by such writers as Lytton Strachey and Garnett, I find an increasing recognition of the claims of French poetry. The old British jibe that the best we can find to say of poetry is that it is *"beau comme la prose"* is losing its hold. You remember that even the most understanding of the English (and the most Francophil) till very recently gave us the palm over themselves for prose, but would not allow us verse. All that is changing, and we seem to be progressing to something like a unity of standard. And perhaps I may be permitted to say that this is the less surprising when we reflect that both Strachey and Garnett write with almost a French discipline. Indeed, when Maurois translated *Lady into Fox* he found that, to all intents and purposes, it translated itself, and, on the other hand, when *Ariel* was translated into English, they tell me, it read like a Lytton Strachey essay.

MYSELF: I shall have a word to say about your Maurois, and our Stracheys and Garnetts, in a minute. But I would just now like to take your point as to the growing understanding between the two peoples. I think that you are right in your belief, and I rejoice that it should be so. But there remains the gulf, which we failed to bridge before dinner. May I put it like this? Your friend asserts that, given genius, your poetry succeeds because of its rules. I, on my side, should assert in spite of them. And I would say in support of this that, though I have never discovered a satisfactory definition of poetry, nor yet any criterion which distinguishes satisfactorily between it and prose, I have always thought of poetry as the " aeroplane touch." I mean by this that at some moment thought lifts from the ground and flies. Now, it is true that birds are liable to all the laws of gravity, but their virtue and beauty is to defy and defeat these laws. You will observe that only three sorts of birds have ever been taught tricks: clumsy ones, like the parrot, the magpie, and the raven; the Pekingese ones, like the canary and pigeon; and birds of prey, like hawks. But nobody has taught the lark or the thrush to sing better or differently, nor has anyone improved on the slow majesty of the swerving gull. Emotional! Yes, but there is a meaning behind it. Flight is no better for clipping the wings. Tell me what your greatest poets have done, and I will tell you why they fall short of Shakespeare's flight and stoop.

F. I. F.: But you are only repeating your St. Cergue trick all over again. You create for us an emotional picture of birds in flight, and then think you have proved your case. Suppose that, as you say, poetry is speech in flight. You admit the laws of gravity. Would the gull fly better if it contravened them? Or the poet because he was reckless of the laws of his craft, as immutable as those of nature? And even if I agreed (though I do not) that Shakespeare is in effect a greater poet than Victor Hugo, I would still say that if he had been a Frenchman he would have learned — what he so abundantly lacked — restraint. And then, perhaps, there would have been no question of his ascendancy.

M. JOCQUELIN: I would rather put it in a different way from my friend. To me, poetry is not, and should not be, primarily a research into the hidden loveliness of words, any more than music of sound. Words are, of course, its raw material, but they should reflect clearly, and, if possible, immutably clear conceptions flashed out at a white heat of creative certainty. You have, I think, in English a phrase " inevitable line." No line is to me inevitable, but the thought behind it may, and indeed should, be.

MYSELF: And there, I believe, we really do come to what the Americans call a " show down." I will confess that it is only in the last two years that I have been able to find what seems to me real poetry in your writers. And shall I tell you what converted me — to what I owed my salvation? It was precisely owing to two lines of Victor Hugo, which seem to me, if any lines in the world are, to be inevitable. They are the last two of the following four:

Votre aile en le heurtant ne fera rien répandre
Du vase, ou je m'abreuve et que j'ai bien rempli.
Mon âme a plus de feu que vous n'avez de cendre;
Mon cœur a plus d'amour que vous n'avez d'oubli.

These two lines have exactly what I seek in true poetry, verbal magic that passes far beyond the poet's mind, and points beyond itself as surely as the arc to the full circle. At its highest moment verse trembles on the edge of thought, and we peer, awe-stricken, over the tall battlements of life.

M. JOCQUELIN: I recognise in what you say the traditional English enthusiasm for lost causes. Victor Hugo

(I say it as a Frenchman) is among the first of our poets, but not because of verbal felicity, though he had that in plenty. But rather because, though he affected to trifle with the rules, he magnificently justified them. He was to a limited extent an innovator, but he never approached within speaking distance of the liberties that the most rigid of English poets habitually allow themselves. It is easy to be an anarchist; but it is terribly difficult to make law and order blossom like the rose. Shakespeare remains to us a triumphant rebel, but Victor Hugo, as it were, makes an archangel out of a policeman.

F. I. F.: I told you he would help me. I could have talked for months and never reached that phrase. In itself it is rather like French poetry. It does, in my mind, decisively present a whole range of ideas in a sentence. It ranges itself definitely, and has the hardness and the many facets of a diamond. Oh! I recognise that it is half a joke, but I am not sure that all poetry may not be, as your proverb has it, a true word spoken in jest. For jest or humour is the sense of proportion reduced to its finest point.

MYSELF: I appreciate both the wit and indeed the profundity of M. Jocquelin's observation. I would only say in reply that I begin to have a glimmering of how a person so gifted and so obviously intelligent as M. Maurois could have committed so formidable a *gaffe* as his *Ariel*. You know, of course, that the book had a wild success in England, probably greater even than it had in France. There were two reasons for this success. In the first place, it was uncommonly well written. It was as lively as Harlequin, and as neatly spangled. In the next place the English are, in matters of literature, amazingly ready to be convinced of the inferiority of their native spirit. Not only that, but at this moment two of their wittiest writers — Strachey and Garnett — were mysteriously convinced of the superiority of all things French. They may deny this: I don't know. But there is hardly a word which they write that hasn't the air of being returned from Cook's with a first-class ticket to the Gare du Nord in its pocket. And these two stand for a great deal in what is most vital in to-day's critical attitude. Like yourselves, they believe in order before beauty, and wit before wisdom. When, therefore, your M. Maurois came along, and presented our radiant Shelley as a sort of man-about-heaven, our literary world emitted a gasp of gratified astonishment. With blistering equanimity M. Maurois ungods our creature of

sunshine, dew and flame,

and converts our demi-god into a *demi-vierge.* The curious thing about it all is that M. André Maurois, unlike so many of his compatriots, actually likes the English. You might have imagined, therefore, that he would have tried to get an English point of view on Shelley. He might, for example, have read Matthew

Arnold on him (though he would have been rather misled by that beautiful essay), or he might actually have read a poem or two by this author. He might, for example, have brooded on "*Adonais,*" or, if he could not have spared time for that, on that single lyric in *Prometheus Unbound,* of which this is the first verse:

> *Life of life! thy lips enkindle*
> *With their love the breath between them.*
> *And thy smiles before they dwindle*
> *Make the cold air fire: then screen them.*
> *In those looks, where whoso gazes*
> *Faints entangled in their mazes.*

He would then have discovered that Shelley's light was of a very formidable character, that it cracked, like a levin-bolt, clean through ugliness, horror, and fear, and that the figure that Maurois described with a certain half-laughing, half-malicious tenderness was as fierce and winged as a Valkyrie. Yes! he could have progressed from Arnold's " beautiful, ineffectual angel " to the true image of one of Milton's Thrones, terrible in its effectual loveliness. I thought, I confess, that the attitude of M. Maurois was dictated partly by sheer in-tellectual flippancy, and partly by the ingrained belief in France that the English were mad as children are mad, not because they are essentially lunatic, but be-cause they aren't yet old enough or civilised enough not to behave as such. But in the light of what you, and M.

Jocquelin, are saying, it seems to me that I have genuinely misjudged M. Maurois. In presenting Shelley as a sort of graceful pantaloon, he was really embodying the theory that poetry is a joke, and consequently that Grock is undoubtedly the greatest living French poet, followed at a respectful distance, in England, by George Robey.

M. JOCQUELIN: You do not, of course, seriously believe what you are saying, nor need I defend my friend, because I see from the look on your face that you know you are being guilty of the very cleverness of which you accuse M. Maurois. But, making allowance for over-emphasis in the heat of controversy, I still remain surprised that you have taken M. Maurois's work so ill. After all, remember that he was not concerned with Shelley's verse, but with his life. If you regard his attitude as flippant, surely it is less so than that of Mr. Lytton Strachey in his Essay on *Cardinal Manning,* which gained, in my view, a so deserved triumph. But we must not let ourselves be distracted from the main issue by Maurois's *tour de force.* You may argue that he has failed to appreciate your Shelley, and conclude, as I understand you said the other evening at dinner apropos of a bottle of Hermitage, " one swallow of this doesn't make a spring: it makes a summer." But you must not let a talent for thinking out epigrams, and delivering them as though they were spontaneous, cloud your vision. Because you are angry with Maurois, you mustn't assume that nobody in France understands English poetry, as you would wish it to be understood. I believe that, if we took half a dozen French and English poets, and chose out what we like best, we should not be far apart. For example, you have chosen *"Puisque j'ai mis ma lèvre"* from Hugo, and I should certainly have chosen *"Adonais"* from Shelley.

F. I. F.: And yet the breach remains unclosed, because even if by accident the two of you lighted on the same poems, and even the same lines, your reasons would be quite different. I remember discussing *Anthony and Cleopatra* once with an Englishman. I asked him what was in his view the highest note of the play, and he quoted the lines of Anthony's return from his pseudo-triumph, when Cleopatra cries:

> *. . . O Lord of Lords,*
> *O infinite virtue, comest thou smiling from*
> *The world's great snare uncaught?*

and Anthony's answer:

> *My nightingale!*

I asked him if he knew José-Maria de Heredia's sonnet of the same name, and, on his admitting ignorance, I gave it him to read. He remained perfectly uninterested, but, at the last three lines, his face lighted up. You remember them, of course:

Et sur elle courbé, l'ardent Imperator
Vit dans ses larges yeux étoilés de points d'or
Toute une mer immense ou fuyaient des galères.

" My God," he said, " if only he'd found the right words, that last line would have been poetry." I don't see how the difference between the two points of view could be more sharply stated. What is it that you English find to be so intoxicated with in the words themselves? What are words? Curious, arbitrary noises, that have, through the process of time, been overlaid either with star-dust or decay. But in themselves nothing. It is the directing vision working through them which is everything. We French seek shape, not coloured clouds.

MYSELF: I am not prepared lightly to abandon either words alone, or in the strange harmonies of rhythm. I believe that, both in themselves, and so grouped, they have a definite objective value. And, indeed, I have often thought that it is the strange superficial lucidity of your words that makes poetry in your language difficult. That gold, elusive essence seems to slip between the smooth surfaces. I can never forget my astonishment and sense of growing estrangement as I read the French Bible. When for our slow, grave, granite words there were substituted your glittering, fish-like shapes, it seemed to me that all the haunting quality had gone. Yes! I will believe, in spite of the whole French Academy and all the French critics since the beginning, that

107

words in themselves have an almost absolute value. Let me give you an example from the living English poet of all others who has demonstrated this. I mean Walter de la Mare; and I will quote one verse, from a poem describing winter, which relies wholly on the unsupported magic of the words themselves:

> *Rilled from her heart the ichor, coursing,*
> *Flamed and awoke her slumbering magic.*
> *Softer than moth's her pinions trembled;*
> *But into blackness, light-like, she fluttered,*
> *Leaving her hollow cold, forsaken.*

> *In air, o'er crystal, rang twangling night-wind,*
> *Bare, rimed pine-woods, murmured lament.*

I have never found that quality in French poetry, and it is my belief that the structure of the language itself forbids it. It seems to me, therefore, that the French theorists, unconsciously recognising this defect in their tongue, have tried to substitute rules for magic. Where the poets have relied on the rules, they have written (to repeat the taunt) poetry as beautiful as prose, and where they have neglected them, or used them as a fence to encourage the legs of Pegasus, they have succeeded, as all poetry everywhere succeeds, by sheer singing magic. But at the very top and climax of all French verse I am still conscious of the reins, and I believe it is, in the last resort, the language itself, and not the rules, that imposes them.

M. Jocquelin: Well! you will hardly expect me to agree with your last conclusion. My view is most clearly that the French language of all media ever created is the best fitted for perfect expression both in prose and verse. It has a suppleness, a lightness, almost a fragrance, and it can assume a Ciceronian pomp or a Demosthenic vehemence with equal effect. But, over and above all, I adhere firmly to Rivarol's famous dictum: "*La langue Française est la seule qui ait une probité attachée a son genie.*" That "probity" of our tongue is exactly what we miss in the Teuton languages, and it seems to me to be reflected in our thought. You said a little earlier, almost eloquently: "At its highest moment verse trembles on the edge of thought, and we peer, awe-stricken, over the tall battlements of life." Well, we French take the view that beyond thought is chaos, and we do not wish to peer over the battlements of life, because there would be nothing to see. We will carry thought to the ends of the earth, but where thought ends there the earth ends. Perhaps this difference is, indeed, fundamental. We have heard much over here of your poetry of the Celtic twilight. I have read in the essays of your W. B. Yeats these phrases: "I see, indeed, in the arts of every country these faint outlines and faint energies . . . which I call the autumn of the body." We French would call it the winter of the mind.

F. I. F.: You see how far apart you are in spite of your hopeful belief that the two of you would ultimately light on the same best poems in the two languages. We shall, I fear, never reach a point when the English will like French poetry for French reasons, or the French, English for English.

MYSELF: Perhaps a thousand years hence, when they are both dead languages!

M. JOCQUELIN: French will never be a dead language!

You are to imagine that by this it was full night, and time for me to descend through the cobbled Cour de St. Pierre, along the Rue de l'Evêque at the side of the Cathedral, down by the Passage des degrés de Poule, through the great hole, and through three hundred years, to the new town. You will forgive me if I linger by the beech-tree for a moment, until the tinkle of the carillon sprays out one o'clock. I should be wondering, I imagine, if we who think that poetry matters most of all, and has an absolute standard, are all fools together. I should be looking defiantly at the little Church of Calvin, very like a spiritual bathing-machine, waiting for a horse to drag it into the waters of controversy. I should be despondent, and then the peace of the square, and the night, and tree, would descend, as palpable as spring rain. And I should go slowly down the *degrés* reciting to myself:

Oh no it is an ever fixéd mark
  That looks on tempests and is never shaken.

It is the star to every wandering bark,
  Whose worth's unknown, although his height be
    taken.

I should go across the bridge where the Rhone flings itself in one green, translucent cataract at the distant sea, and, as I step into the Bergues, I should say to myself: " M. Jocquelin was right in saying that it would never be a dead language. But he should have said English."

THE DIFFICULTIES
OF THE POET

The Difficulties of the Poet

A PRELIMINARY QUESTION, which I shall for the moment burk, is to determine what is a poet and what is poetry. Eighty years ago that question would have answered itself — a poet is Mr. Alfred Tennyson, and poetry is what he writes; while, if negative assurances were desired, Browning and *Sordello* were available. But the matter is no longer so simple. The age of eminence and pre-eminence has — thank God! — passed. No single figure with a resolutely romantic appearance blots out the literary sky. The sky is full of a tumult of clouds no bigger than a man's hand, and often, indeed, no more formidable than a woman's. Whatever our skill in meteorological prediction, we cannot affirm, for example, that the faintly self-satisfied depression which has so long hung over Bloomsbury will necessarily involve all of us in its own patient and perhaps tepid drizzle. We cannot assume that a Sitwellian anti-cyclone will assure a period of fine, if rather paradoxical, weather. We cannot assert that Mr. Chesterton in the habit of Boreas, or Mr. de la Mare as the soft west wind, will necessarily prevail. Nor need we apprehend that the violent atmospheric disturbance in the higher critical centres of the apostles of "modernist" verse will permanently substitute the noise of falling rafters for the liquid freedom of Shelley's rising skylark.

Indeed, as in so many other directions in this puzzled post-war world, we have no certain guides and no definite goals. We are all acutely conscious of a change in values. We find it hard to believe that there could have been anything estimable and worthy of emulation in a period so demented as to precipitate and to permit the precipitation of the Great War. Above all, we are convinced that the poets who fiddled gently anæmic appreciations of the hero, when the world that he died in vain to save was burning, should be banished for ever from the memory of man. Even the legendary figure of Rupert Brooke "into cleanness leaping" is a warning of how what is loveliest and best may be betrayed by the coolly abominable dithyrambs of bewildered politicians, rather than an example of youth triumphant over death. "There's not a corner of a foreign field but is for ever England," murmur the disillusioned voices of those who survived, adding, "that with all the other advantages of England it will comprise an unemployment figure of 1,000,000, stag-hunting, and the Rothermere Press." "Yes," these voices observe, "a fitting rider to that sonnet would be such lines as:

> *"Within an English graveyard snore*
> *The business men who won the war,*

While by the foreign seas they crossed, it
Happens lie the men who lost it."

You will not wonder then if in a world so vexed and wracked the poet — who is, or should be, the apostle of peace — is, quite apart from difficulties of technique, face to face with an almost overwhelming difficulty in point of subject-matter. He may well conclude that the day of half-lights with W. B. Yeats and side-lights with de la Mare are over. Ireland has, he may urge, exchanged the children of Usna for the Shannon Scheme, and the musicianers of Araby have been driven into confused flight by the loud trumpets of Colonel Lawrence and the reverberant thumpings of his successive drummers. He may ask himself, too, whether there is still refuge in the mild pastures of Georgia. Can he reasonably recapture the first fine careless rapture of the milk-pail, or, with Mr. Harold Monro, celebrate the endearing vagaries of kitchen utensils? If he feels that not even Mr. Blunden can justify the return to Wordsworth, where is he to look? The verse that welcomed the war died in the mud and stench of the battlefields. The bitter beauty of Siegfried Sassoon and Wilfred Owen —

Hearts, you are not so hot
As hearts made great with shot —

bursts like an immortal shell. What remains? Where shall he look?

The obvious answer (though not, as I shall hope to show, the true answer) is satire. The poet may well urge that the only thing to do with a world so foul is to wring its neck, and that poetry, by virtue of its eternal economies, is best equipped to perform this execution. It will hardly be straight satire — like that written by Pope. It will be satire which will exemplify in its own form the declensions that it derides. Thus two considerable poets, T. S. Eliot and Herbert Read, of set purpose carry their criticism of the formlessness of contemporary life into the formlessness of their verse. If Eliot thinks of a nightingale singing " jug-jug " — as in the earliest of all English poems — he will round off the song by observing that it is directed " to dirty ears." If he writes a poem so beautiful as:

She and the lady in the cape
Are suspect, thought to be in league;
Therefore the man with heavy eyes
Declines the gambit, shows fatigue,

Leaves the room and reappears
Outside the window, leaning in;
Branches of wistaria
Circumscribe a golden grin;

The host with someone indistinct
Converses at the door apart,
The nightingales are singing near
The Convent of the Sacred Heart,

> *And sang within the bloody wood*
> *When Agamemnon cried aloud,*

he will end it:

> *And let their liquid siftings fall*
> *To stain the stiff dishonoured shroud,*

thereby deliberately smashing his own beauty, and throwing good poetry after bad conditions of existence. And Herbert Read will write:

> *But once upon a time*
> *The oakleaves and the wild boars —*
> *Antonio, Antonio,*
> *The old wound is bleeding.*

> *We are in Silvertown;*
> *We have come here with a modest ambition*
> *To know a little bit about the river,*
> *Eating cheese and pickled onions on a terrace by the*
>   *Thames.*

He throws, you see, cheese and pickled onions with a gesture of infinite weariness straight into the flushed and shining face of Euterpe. Nothing, he maintains, matters now. There was a beauty of the wild boar in the wood. He will not imitate the dulcet pities of

> *Nous n'irons plus aux bois. Les lauriers*
>   *sont coupés.*

If the laurel-trees are uprooted, he will strike down the gold and laurelled head too. We shall have satire not only on the world, but on verse itself, the everlasting disinfectant. And when the disinfectant has been infected, how shall it be disinfected?

Must the poet, like these two, frankly accept the domination of despair, must he cry that verse was once prose in flight, not from reality, but into it, healing and consecrating? Poetry was once the moment when what is pedestrian in us lifts its heron-wings for the lazy flight into immortality. Must he acknowledge that now reality is a clumsy shambles in which verse, with all the other deluded cattle of mortality, falls under the hammer of a blind and drunken butcher? Must he admit that, so far from wings rising, we have the thud, as in Osbert Sitwell's poem, of grouse butchered to make an aristocrat's or a profiteer's holiday!

But if he will not admit any of that, where is he to look? To Psyche perhaps, but not to Edgar Allan Poe's Psyche:

> *Helen, thy beauty is to me*
> *Like those Nicæn barks of yore,*
> *That gently, o'er a perfumed sea,*
> *The weary, wayworn wanderer bore*
> *To his own native shore.*
>
> *On desperate seas long wont to roam,*
> *Thy hyacinth hair, thy classic face,*

Thy Naiad airs, have brought me home
To the glory that was Greece
And the grandeur that was Rome.

Lo! in yon brilliant window-niche
How statue-like I see thee stand,
The agate lamp within thy hand!
Ah, Psyche, from the regions which
Are Holy Land!

No, not a Psyche leaning up through space with the young, star-troubled Eros, but a Freudian Psyche, a Psyche of that crawling, unholiest land on the boundaries of lust and lunacy. Will the poet, by descending there, like Dante into Inferno, like Æneas into Avernus, bring back consolation from under the very brows of death? There is one poet — Robert Graves:

Small gnats that fly
In hot July
And lodge in sleeping ears,
Can rouse therein
A trumpet's din
With Day-of-Judgment fears.

Small mice at night
Can wake more fright
Than lions at midday;
A straw will crack
The camel's back,
There is no easier way.

> *One smile relieves*
> *A heart that grieves*
> *Though deadly sad it be,*
> *And one hard look*
> *Can close the book*
> *That lovers love to see.*

He has come back — that gay traveller — heavily burdened and limping under his load. His song has for the moment (let us hope for the moment only) dried in his own throat, and his ears, accustomed to the inchoate babblings of those evil shades, tune themselves to a queer, unnatural echo of that dissolute utterance, as when he praises a writer such as E. E. Cummings.

He will even palter with Gertrude Stein, who, for me, has reduced the English language to a series of uncontrollable hiccoughs. It seems at least doubtful whether here is a resting-place for the poet's feet.

Should the poet, then, instead of adventuring behind the utmost edge of reality, deliberately turn his back on it, and invent with Edith Sitwell a new, fresh-coloured world by its side, inhabited not by men and women, but by brightly painted wooden toys? That is no doubt a possible, even a brilliant, way out, but it is strictly individual. It will only be open to an adventurer for whom, as for Miss Sitwell, the three notes of reality become, not like Browning's fourth note, a star, but a fourth dimension. But even Miss Sitwell appears to be a little homesick for earth in her strange Paradise.

In her latest (and most beautiful) volume she writes
thus of a mother murdered by her son:

> *He stole to kill me while I slept,*
> *The little son who never wept*
> *But that I kissed his tears away*
> *So fast, his weeping seemed but play.*
>
> *So light his footfall. Yet I heard*
> *Its echo in my heart and stirred*
> *From out my weary sleep to see*
> *My child's face bending over me.*
>
> *The wicked knife flashed serpent-wise,*
> *Yet I saw nothing but his eyes*
> *And heard one little word he said*
> *Go echoing down among the Dead.*

This is a very different world from that of:

> *Through gilded trellises*
> *Of the heat, Dolores,*
> *Inez, Manuccia,*
> *Isobel, Lucia,*
> *Mock Time that flies.*
>
> . . . .
>
> *Through gilden trellises*
> *Of the heat, spangles*
> *Pelt down through the tangles*
> *Of bell-flowers; each dangles*

Her castanets, shutters
Fall while the heat mutters,
With sounds like a mandoline
Or tinkled tambourine. . . .
Ladies, Time dies.

It seems, doesn't it, as though Miss Sitwell, like Mr. Robert Graves, were coming back, but, unlike him, not burdened, but enfranchised for the contemplation of mortal agony and mortal beauty. And it would almost seem as though she herself were declaring that there is no Sitwellian road to learning reality.

Where, then, shall the poet turn? I spoke of satire before only to dismiss it, but principally because the two poets, whom I quoted, had twined the satire in their own work. There might perhaps be room for satire, like that of Hilaire Belloc and Chesterton, which, without sacrificing its own form, does flay the world. Indeed, in the Preface to a little book of squibs of my own called *Lampoons* I put forward a plea for satire in verse:

"I daresay that in all these respects the age resembles all its predecessors. I don't know. I have only lived in this one. I am content to leave the dead to bury their dead. I reserve my indignation and hate for what can at least be abused, if it cannot be altered. And it is one of the most significant features of a time when it is supremely the case that *difficile est saturam non scribere,* that nobody writes satire of the plain, old-fashioned type, which raged with Juvenal, Rabelais, Pope, and Swift. We have, it is true, Bernard Shaw, Chesterton, and, trundling after them at a long interval, Hilaire Belloc. But Bernard Shaw's satire, terrible, relentless, and final as it is, lays an axe at the root of the world. He will hew down the crooked old tree, Ygdrasil, and plant a clean young fir in its place. For that very reason his is a struggle of the high gods, and the bolts in that huge contest are as high above us, if as dazzling, as the lightning. Shaw is a figure in the Twilight of the Gods, and he is the one thing between Valhalla and the grim beasts crawling to its destruction. He is, therefore, not so much a new satirist as a new religion.

"Chesterton and Belloc, on the other hand, do definitely (and most satisfactorily) hate what comes under their observation. But their observation is limited (in this regard) to Jews, and politicians who, if they are not Jews, very well might be. Though I may perhaps be excused from sharing their opinions in this matter, I can, as one who feels that an ounce of clean hatred is worth a ton of impertinent indulgence, rejoice in such stuff as:

" We also know the sacred height
  Upon Tugela side,
Where those three hundred fought with Beit,
  And fair young Wernher died.

" The daybreak on the failing force,
The final sabres drawn:
Tall Goltman, silent on his horse,
Superb against the dawn.

" Or in —

" Two straight lines
Can't enclose a space,
But they can enclose a Corner to support the Chosen
Race.

" But the fact remains that the world is not wholly inhabited by Jews and politicians, and that it might be more profitable if these writers would hit a man of their own size (if, indeed, one could be discovered!). I mean by this that it has generally been found much easier to hate a Jew and a politician than anybody else. To pummel the Jew, who, by reason of his historical position, has always one hand tied behind his back, even if the other is in your pocket, is a queer way of exhibiting your strength, and as for the politician, you might as well hammer a figure of speech, or, rather, that is exactly what you are hammering. There await attack, smug, easy and unmolested, a thousand things infinitely less vulnerable, and far more in need of being hit and hurt. Why will no one attack them, and attack them in the most effective medium of all-verse ? "

I have since then in a book called *News of the Devil* carried my precept into practice, and I will, if I may, read a passage illustrating the argument that follows:

" War! devil! There is something I remember
out of the world in which I lived. September
through all the fields of France with apple and corn
drifted and dreamed. Morn followed dew-rich morn
with gradual wealth, and the soft silver eves
played Harlequin across the golden leaves.
And while the immemorial harvester
garnered her sheaves, a shadow followed her,
and as she, smiling, whispered 'It is good,'
out of the air a hellish multitude
leaped at her shoulder, yelling as they tore,
'Murder and blood! The harvest-home of war,'
Listen! I can remember something else
I wrote of this, 'War has its miracles
of high regeneration and release
more than the milky benefits of peace.
Men find their souls in battle, having lost them,
nations their hearts, whatever war may cost them.
Strike for the right! Let everything go in.
One touch of murder makes the whole world kin.'
These things I wrote. Outside my window went
on steady feet a marching regiment.
I threw aside the curtain. Shrill and airy
they piped 'The long, long way to Tipperary,'
the short, short way to death, and, as they played,

across the centuries an echo strayed:
' Te morituri salutamus.' Yes!
I saw my chosen gladiators pass
like Cæsar, and like Cæsar turn the thumb,
and heard between the bugle and the drum,
a Roman crying to an English lad:
' We died for Cæsar! Wherefore are you dead?'
and heard the English voice make answer, ' Nay!
we die to make a Pressman's holiday.'
I say I heard. I lie. I did not hear it.
Only to-day deep in my wounded spirit
I understand what meant the sudden cry
' Paul Arthur. That's Paul Arthur.' They passed by
cheering my name, and, as they cheered, I swore
to dedicate myself to them and war
as to a faith, and, turning to my desk,
I wrote, ' Whatever this high cause may ask
it must be given, as a lover gives,
freely.' ' Who dies,' I wrote, ' if Arthur lives?'

" ' Arthur!' the devil whispered, tempting yet.
' Freedom! not Arthur. Surely you forget.'
' Aye, freedom,' answered Arthur, ' is a name
that covers up a multitude of shame.
Freedom for whom? For what? They did not guess
who died, and I, who lived for it, still less.
We who believed we moulded to a pattern
the world, but split it, like a clumsy slattern
dropping a dish, and when the dish was smashed,

we said this was exactly what we wished.
Some lived for freedom, and ten millions died
to win or keep it, and, for all we tried,
like two blind beggars fighting for a penny,
we woke to find there never had been any.
But for myself, I hear, I always hear,
devil, the thin, the terrible soft cheer
of the faithful dead who died, that liberty
might die with them. And all day long I see
faces, faint faces, cold, innumerable,
that smiled on me in passing, knowing well
there is no laughter in death (and as a child
puzzled, but trusting me, they passed and smiled).
Aye, they march through my heart in dreams, the living
patient, most ignorant, and most forgiving.
They smile, and pass, and fade, and here I stand
in no man's company, in No Man's Land.
O God, I fought with you, and with your stars,
See, God, how deep my wounds, and all my scars.'"

I said that I would quote these lines not for their own sake but as an illustration. At the time when I wrote them I did not feel that denunciation was the key to this age for the poet. I thought that along with all other artists it was his duty to expose the clumsy muddle of massacre and spite that was called War; that it was supremely his business to strip off the flimsy veils of pseudo-romance, to demonstrate that there is a price too high to pay where dishonour is at stake — the price not only of young untarnished lives, but still more of young untarnished dreams. The wounds that I believed it was his mission to explore were not those of death or of pain, but the wound in the mind — the malady inflicted by the poison-gas of war that converts some of us into something rich and strangely like a devil, some into vicarious assassins of gentleness, beauty and delight, and all of us into creatures of primitive and mud-like emotions and instincts. But I came to see, as I see now, that hate may blast but it cannot heal, it may amputate but it cannot restore the blood to a drooping limb. There is, and always must be, a place for the true satirist, by which I mean one who, knowing himself no better than his fellows, exposes his own weaknesses, and elevates that exposure into a universal demonstration. Nor do I waver in the belief that verse, because of its brilliant economy of form, is ultimately the most effective and perhaps the most enduring instrument of satire. But I am coming to the conclusion that there is no royal road to spurning the world. The poet must never, like Wordsworth, complain that

The world is too much with us.

He must drench himself in its turbid waters, and, if he drowns, at least he will have heard the dark sea-horns of the abyss.

You will see, therefore, that I have reached a point at which, after exploring all the new paths in Parnassus, I take refuge in generalities. But if I am driven to admit that the poet's task does not change from age to age, that it remains in part that of the universal vindicator, in part that of the common apologist, the difficulties of the medium to be selected are still to be faced. That will bring me for a brief moment to a consideration of technique, and I shall have to ask myself and you whether the traditional forms of verse are in fact obsolete, and whether we must from this dispense, not only with all the French forms, not only with the sonnet, but even with the native measures of blank verse and the heroic couplet.

As with their subject-matter, so with their form the poets of to-day have their special difficulties. For many of them the traditional forms have a romantic association alien to the times. None of them can conceive themselves like Austin Dobson, or in much less degree like Andrew Lang and Edmund Gosse succeeding with the rondeau, the ballade, or the vilanelle. They would as soon entrust their bodies to a sedan-chair, or their heads to a wig-maker. But it is not only these self-consciously tripping and elegant modes that embarrass them. The poets are convinced that they must be both in the world and of it. How, then, can a sonnet summarise the emotions of an American millionaire on first seeing an adding-machine, or still more of an adding-machine on first seeing that multiplying machine in the flesh? Isn't it likely, they urge, that, as life spreads and sprawls, verse must spread with it, if not actually sprawl in its company? It is true, they admit, that Masefield, and even Ezra Pound have used the sonnet form, but only to reject it, the former for the heroic couplet deliberately rendered unheroic, the latter for verse so free as to be poetically licentious. All predigested harmonies are, they believe, foreign to a totally undigested (and almost indigestible) period.

For that reason, even so characteristically an English measure as blank verse is suspect. Contemporary life does not scan, and to interpose rhythm is necessarily to muffle or mislead it. The poet therefore tends to welcome the Transatlantic invasion. Not without reason does that portentous figure proclaim Liberty at the entrance of New York Harbour, not in vain does she turn her back on the country from which that commodity is exported. We seek, therefore, to live up to Carl Sandburg who writes:

> *It is cold*
> *The bitter of the winter*
> *Whines a story.*
> *It is the colder weather when the truck*
> *Drivers sing, it would freeze the whiskers*
> *Off a brass monkey.*
> *It is the bitterest whining of the winter now.*

Or we seek to reach the dazzling simplicities of H. P. when with all that Greek certainty of craft she writes:

> *No, it isn't true,*
> *they're not all horrible;*

You're always unfair.
Well, there you see,
we quarrel again;
don't talk — dismiss happiness,
Unhappiness, pain, bliss,
even thought.

We invoke the saxophone, or the factory hooter in place of the pipe and the harp: we substitute Walt Whitman for William Shakespeare.

It is therefore reasonable to ask whether the poet is right to be so deflected, just as in the world of pictures there are those who venture to enquire whether that canvas which least reproduces the object of sight is the supreme achievement. The answer in both cases is, I suppose, yes and no. Yes, in so far as a creative artist has found a new and satisfactory medium. No, if that medium is deliberately adopted as an escape from difficulties. The writer of free verse will only be justified if he can produce in the mind of the reader the sense of distant and lonely song. These are the three sovereign elements — distance, loneliness, and singing. If he achieves these three (and T. S. Eliot in the poem I read seems to me to achieve them) he will have succeeded, whatever shape his verse assumes: if he fail, not all the devices of typography will save him. And it will not follow that poets cannot be found to-day or hereafter to whom the traditional forms will be natural, who will evoke new and lovelier genies out of the old age-sweetened bottles. We need not doubt that a new W. B. Yeats, a later de la Mare, or a resurgent Ralph Hodgson might demonstrate that there are still a million unguessed rhythms in the decasyllable, a million rose-leaves in the rhyme. Spring, after all, works with the old material — a clod of earth, a dead branch, and two blades of grass, and each year she achieves this much with means so slender. And what Spring can do with dead wood, shall not Primavera achieve in the soul with dead forms and dead rhythms? Who knows how soon, wandering in the bare ruined choirs, we may not see the first green shadow that will prove that one more poet has overcome the everlasting and beautiful impossibilities of verse?

PUBLIC SERVANTS
IN FICTION

Public Servants in Fiction

Milton concluded his justly celebrated defence of blindness by observing that

They also serve who only stand and wait.

It is true that the poet was, superficially at any rate, referring to his own tragic loss of sight, but this will not deceive the acute reader. Milton had, of course, a long and distinguished career as a Civil Servant. We are therefore entitled to assume (and if we aren't I shall assume none the less) that when he spoke of blindness he was thinking not primarily of physical, but of spiritual blindness — that mental condition which leads a man, otherwise in possession of his four remaining senses, to adopt the Civil Service as a career. Having brooded with increasing despondency on the disadvantages of that situation, with the most magnificent gesture of optimism on record, he consoles the victim by his assurance that " standing and waiting " is also service. It will be observed, however, that his optimism does not lead him into indiscretion. He does not dwell on the one hand upon what the Public Servant has to " stand," nor on the other hand does he indicate what he is waiting for. He merely congratulates him generally upon his inevitable vicissitudes in both directions, believing, as a poet is entitled to believe, that misfortune is an end in itself.

We have here, therefore, the first portrait of a Civil or Public Servant with which I am acquainted. For, since I do not include Ministers of the Crown in that description, I cannot avail myself of Shakespeare's Wolsey. Had this not been so, I might have permitted myself to speculate whether the episode of the misdirection of the list of the Cardinal's property might not have been a covert attack upon the Registry, that Department so often and so unjustly accused of having mislaid the files relating to civilisation. Nor am I prepared to accept Polonius as a person who would be qualified for membership of the Institute of Public Administration. For, though a tendency to agree with the apparently inconsistent decisions of his Chief — Hamlet — might lay him open to this charge, I do not believe (in spite of what has no doubt been urged by many German commentators) that this is what Shakespeare really had in mind. Nor do I accept the view that when Hamlet referred (a trifle injudiciously) to " the insolence of office " that Shakespeare was concerned with the Inland Revenue Department of the day. No, we must come to the conclusion that Shakespeare, having exhausted his powers of tragic endurance in the plays culminating in *King Lear,* deliberately turned aside from the life of the Civil Servant, which he may well have regarded as surpassing the limits

138

of the pity and terror that a true artist is entitled to use.

In accepting the thesis that the life of the Public Servant is one in the high tragic vein, I am not basing myself upon the few facts relating to it that have come under my personal notice. I am, I hope, too experienced an administrator to be misled by facts. I am dealing with the life of the Public Servant as I find it in such fiction as has come my way. I might begin, perhaps, with Mr. Trollope's glimpses of persons, who can only be excused on the ground that they have been dead such a long time, and end with the endearing portraiture of Messrs. Poy and McCartney, whose figures can be justified on the ground that they never existed except in their authors' minds, and that even that existence, having regard to its slender origins, must be regarded as precarious. But, when I do face the Public Servant as so portrayed, I confess that I am conscious of the dark and persistent shape of tragedy, drooping remorselessly and indeed expansively, if I may use the phrase, " all over the shop." For what is the general, the composite, picture of the Public Servant which evolves itself from these sources? There are, in fact, two main streams of representation what I may call the mandarin-cum-parasite, and, on the other hand, the type relegated to imprisonment for life in the Second Division. The first of these types is fairly uniform. He is distinguished by equal imbecility and callousness. Indeed his only pretension to articulate intellect is displayed in the low cunning with which he adheres to his post. He is a barnacle, or, as the more reticent wit of our generation puts it, a limpet. Like that furtive shellfish, his life's business is to stick, for no particular purpose, to obscure and unlighted portions of the public ship. (I do not apologise for the use of this phrase, because it has now been settled, by general agreement, that the omission of this metaphor in any sustained reference to the State argues the performer to be devoid of all acquaintance with the subject.) But, like the shellfish, our limpet is not only adhesive and secretive, he has a fishlike absence of mind, and he has this particular fish's quality of hardness. If you set about the limpet, you are liable to bruise your knuckles, and at the end to find that nothing has been accomplished. Nor must " you " in this connection be identified only with the public, the master of this peculiarly unsatisfactory servant, but " you " is to include the non-mandarin. The harshness of the mandarin to his employer is only exceeded by his brutality to his faithful subordinate, upon whose wits he battens. This subordinate, though mentally he may

. . . *sew*
yard upon yard of calico

all coloured red, and though he may be swathed in it to that extent that he is spared the necessity of buying new suits, yet he alone performs any negligible fraction of administration that is actually achieved. He

140

combines with the entanglements of Laocoön the burden of Atlas, except that the world which he supports is really a desiccated orange. But, infinitely contemptible and dried as it is, he alone staggers under its weight. The mandarin walks behind him lashing him forward to that bourne from which no traveller returns, because in this case he never reaches it. These are the types: on the one hand a fool, jobbed in by criminal aunts, weakly vicious, and completely ignorant of the purpose and meaning of government; on the other, pale, wan, and constant, the devoted Morlock, bent to the ground by domestic embarrassment and public injury, emerging from his deep underground pits where he labours in darkness, to tremble in the unfamiliar moonlight, shed by the minds of successive limners of the Public Servant. And, meantime, the great art of Government, draped like a Greek player, broods apart, unrecognised and forgotten. . . . . .

I have put in these full-stops so that nobody may doubt that a dramatic climax of the first order has been reached — a long tragic pause in which you are asked to envisage the shapes in conflict of the art of Government and the two Public Servants. It was because I had this tremendous dichotomy in mind that I hinted that Shakespeare had faltered, yes, had not dared to snatch the veil aside. " My public," he would probably explain to Kit Marlowe (if he happened to be alive at the time) — " My public can stand two lovers dying exquisitely in one tomb, they can endure Kent's ' vile jellies ' reft from his forehead, they can sit through Lady Macbeth's outcry to the dagger, they can with hearts unwrung hear Desdemona's tale that begins 'My mother had a maid called Barbara,' and they can confront Egypt's 'immortal longings.' But this, Kit," he would say, "— well I put it to you. Is it or isn't it caviare? " And if Shakespeare avoided the theme it may (though I hope it will not) be objected that I might perhaps be well advised to leave it alone. I will not deny that this is an objection which I have more than once felt, in the course of writing this paper, to be well-founded. I have consoled myself with the well-known aphorism that a Civil Servant not only does not know when he is beaten, but frequently does not know when he is dead —and I have proceeded in that belief.

Nor is the matter one wholly for frivolous treatment. In the *Republic* of Plato — one of the most beautiful books that even that master of loveliness contrived — the art of administration or of government is handled. It seemed to Plato that the highest privilege to which any citizen could aspire, as indeed, because of its intrinsic ardours, the least coveted, was that of government. It did not seem to him that the arts of war were the most commendable; of the creative arts he was doubtful, since he would not have the Ionian strains in his city; business he did not recognise so much as an art as the occupation of slaves; and of the Press he had not heard. To him, beset (or perhaps fortified) by these ignorances and prejudices, it seemed that in good administration was to be found the art of life itself. He drew with loving detail a Celestial City and his Celestial Citizens occupied themselves with the duty of governing as eagerly as among us citizens less celestial engage in commercial avocations. The governors did not apologise for governing, nor were they despised for it. So arduous was the task that rulers were self-chosen by virtue of assuming, almost against their will, the burden imposed upon them by their own high characters. In a word, in Plato's City the Public Servant was a shadow of the παραδειγμα εν τοις ουρανοις.

It is not the purpose of this paper to inquire how the change of attitude to the Public Service has come about, nor to speculate why those who are occupied with what in the end matters most to everybody should be so scolded and blamed. It may be, perhaps, that Englishmen, unlike Greeks, do not need to be governed, or it may be that the Englishman is incapable of governing. It may be that fiction, whether represented by Mr. Trollope or the *Evening News,* does not reflect the true attitude of Englishmen to their Public Servants. It may even be that the English, who in the ordinary relations of life are, above all other nations, patient, tolerant and just, do not change radically in this one relation. Fortunately, I need not engage myself in these speculations, for I am concerned with fiction. But I could not bring myself to display to you the disheartening chronicle of the

Public Servant in fiction without indicating in advance this curious outstanding fact. You will find in fiction noble and ignoble soldiers, sailors, doctors and lawyers, and noble or ignoble often by virtue of their professional excellence or ignominy. But the Public Servant is uniform in colour and drawing, so that when William Morris, for example, constructs his Celestial City, he achieves it by omitting government (and Public Servants) altogether.

The obvious place at which to begin, I suppose, is " The Circumlocution Office " in Dickens' *Little Dorrit,* because Dickens in a noisy, splendid way, like a large man spashing in a small bath, did drench the Public Servant, and gave him a cold in the head (and in the heart) from which he has not yet recovered. Now, in explaining and understanding this attitude, two things must not be forgotten. In the first place, Charles Dickens was a social reformer, who really felt what was evil as a personal injury, and really hit it clean and hard. In the second place, one is at liberty to guess that the Public Service of the day was a thing that deserved hitting. The first of these points requires a momentary further examination only because of a comfortable belief that the Victorian era was, on the whole, a noble and uplifting period in our history. It would, I think, be truer to say (though this may savour of hyperbole) that it was, on the whole, worse than our own period, and it would certainly be true to say it would have been a great deal worse if it had not been for Dickens. For

Dickens was that extraordinarily rare type of genius which could express lasting truths in music-hall phraseology. Dickens was, indeed, a cartoonist using a method not unlike that practised by " Poy," whom I have already mentioned. He chose, that is to say, some easily recognisable object, inflated it, attached a label to it, and then set it out on its travels in a shape as permanent as that of a big doll. The difference, however, between Dickens and " Poy " is that, whereas " Poy's " figures continue to have the appearance of dummies whose producer speaks (and who apparently thinks) with the stomach, the figures of Dickens burst into life at such a speed that they almost get out of our sight in their race for immortality. When the figure was intended to symbolise a whole set of conditions the result was as conclusive as it was often disagreeable. Sairey Gamp smashed the thieving, gin-swilling generation of nurses, not only because she is a miracle of true English humour, nor because the humour threw so grim a flashlight on grave abuses, but also because of her constant use of one phrase: " Vich, Mrs. 'Arris, I ses." That phrase has the universality of " Yes, we have no bananas "; but it is, in Dickens' hands, as though the phrase had been pronounced, as his contribution to the problem of disarmament, by the President of the United States.

Dickens chose to wield this terrific weapon against the Public Service, as he had wielded it against the delays of Chancery, the shams of Doctors' Commons, the

Yorkshire schoolmaster, and the parish beadle. Now, in every one of these cases, his indignation was justly aroused, and the chastisement amply deserved. I will content myself with expressing the hope that in respect of the Civil Servant he was misinformed. But, whether he was misinformed or not, he has presented a picture of Red Tape, of callous indifference to justice and honour, of ignorance, of nepotism, of sheer overwhelming machine-like stupidity that has not been wholly erased from the canvas of the Civil Service in the sixty odd years since it was written. Fortunately (or, rather, unfortunately) the account of the Circumlocution Office and of the Barnacle family is so generally and so intimately known that I shall not need to devote much space to it. But I may, perhaps, select one or two phrases which indicate how Dickens drove his cartoon home. First, then, of the Office itself he says, " Whatever was required to be done, the Circumlocution Office was beforehand with all the public departments in the art of perceiving — ' How not to do it.' These last five words, being the " Yes, we have no bananas " motive, are printed in capitals. But it does not stop there. Dickens does not trust his public to absorb the phrase in one. He repeats it eight times in the next three pages, and each time it clinches a paragraph or phrase with ringing bitterness. By the time, after three pages of brilliant repetition, we reach the Barnacle family, the nail has not only been hit on the head, but it has been hit into the reader's head. Having now

146

firmly grasped the simple truth that the art of Government is, in fact, not to govern, we are introduced to Clarence Barnacle, son of Tite Barnacle, a high official in the office, cousin of Ferdinand Barnacle, who is private secretary to Lord Decimus Tite Barnacle, a person of whose actual position, in relation to the Office, Dickens appears to be in doubt, and who, though so named, he seems to believe to be a peer. But, putting that on one side, we have four Barnacles (to say nothing of the Stillstalkings in the background), and, though no capital letters have been used, we have somehow or other been led to realise that nepotism is an outstanding feature of the Public Service. In the matter of imbecility, however, Dickens does not use the mace. Being a genius of the first order, he has a perfect armoury of weapons, and he now selects a rapier with a blade almost as fine and as hard as a dentist's drill. Barnacle Junior is confronted with a member of the public who has had the temerity to invade the Office without an appointment. Let us hear the description of the rising Civil Servant: " He had a superior eye-glass dangling round his neck, but, unfortunately, had such flat orbits to his eyes, and such limp little eyelids that it wouldn't stick in when he put it up." The member of the public desires to discuss the affairs of a debtor who has been in the Marshalsea prison for about a quarter of a century (during which time it would appear the papers in his case have been lost in the Registry). Mr. Barnacle is at first divided between the agonies of coping with his eye-glass and those caused by the discovery that the member of the public has no appointment. He thaws, however, to the point of crying:

" But, I say. Look here! Is this public business? " and, receiving an ambiguous reply, continues:

" Is it anything about — Tonnage — or that sort of thing? "

Swinburne in a moment of excitement observed that one of Dickens' characters undid a button and passed into immortality. Mr. Barnacle is safe in the same haven with his tonnage.

From Barnacle Junior the member of the public is deflected to the private house of Barnacle Senior — Tite Barnacle. Mr. Barnacle, Senior, is suddenly and violently revealed: " He seemed to have been sitting for his portrait to Sir Thomas Lawrence all the days of his life." Here we leave the area of the rapier. Mr. Barnacle is — by virtue of about 32 hyphens interposed in his sentences — the embodiment of Red Tape. After, in the most hyphenated manner, having failed to give his applicant any information, he (hyphen) refers him (hyphen) to, in fact (hyphen), the Circumlocution (pronounced as though it had five and twenty syllables) Office. On return to the Office we are introduced to Callous Rudeness and Puppyish Insolence in the person of Mr. Wobbler and his friend, who prefer to discuss the antics of a hocussed dog to those of the by now three parts hocussed member of the public. On being sent elsewhere he is, however, called back to hear, " Shut the door after you. You're letting in a devil of a draught here." Finally the stunned member of the public is brought up against the one bright Barnacle, who explained "the Department to be a politico-diplomatic hocus-pocus piece of machinery for the assistance of the nobs in keeping off the snobs."

There is a good deal more, but we may leave it there. Dickens had given the Public Service their niche in the minds of their fellow countrymen, so that half a century later, when the play of *Barnacles* was revised under the name of *Limpets,* everybody was prepared to applaud, and it was certain of a good run.

After Dickens, Trollope. Trollope, in my view, is a writer of merit who is at the moment running the risk of being damned by a sudden revival of interest in him. He is being praised by persons infinitely cleverer than was this excellent Post Office Surveyor for qualities which he not only did not possess, but would have repudiated, if necessary, in a three-volume disclaimer. The fact about Trollope, as I see him, is that he is one of the few persons who, without any literary gifts, wrote (on occasion) literature. His style is not merely execrable: it simply doesn't exist. His technique is that of a shop assistant cutting off lengths of material. As an artist he would have given Flaubert indigestion, and have hastened de Maupassant's intellectual tragedy.

And when all that has been said it remains true that he is one of the best tellers of a story that we have in English. His people are never witty, noble, or wise;

they are not romantic, or sinister; they suffer no extremities of joy or sorrow; they are content simply with living. One drifts into their company as into a vicarage tea-party. At the tea-party nothing happens, or could happen, because what we are sharing is the surface of life, not its springs. But the surface is a part of life, indeed with many the whole of life. If, therefore, the surface can be reproduced life has been reproduced, and this, with a queer, warm, unfaltering shrewdness and mellow grown-upness of outlook, Trollope unfalteringly captures. So much is this the case that it might even be urged that the very formlessness of his was part of a deliberate scheme. That would be an ingenious theory, but almost certainly a wrong one. The form of his work, I am convinced, is due to its having been written largely in trains in between the composition and reading of official memoranda. He seeks to be as unlike an official as he can, and he notably succeeds. But all the time, while I am conscious of this incorrigible sloppiness, I feel a level, gentle, but essentially masculine intelligence brooding happily, but not profoundly, on the gentle ranges of life spread before him. He keeps looking out of the railway carriage window and seeing an amiable country landscape. He returns to his paper and notes it down.

It is not to be expected that in such a writer we shall find repeated the savage indignations and equally savage insight of Dickens. Trollope's Public Servant will be a normal mid-Victorian citizen first, and a

Public Servant second. For, after all, Trollope, a Civil Servant himself, no doubt took himself in that order. But, though this was to be expected, yet it is none the less remarkable how shadowy the picture of the Public Service is. When Trollope concerns himself with Barchester, you can almost hear the cathedral bells and the slow feet of Mr. Hardinge dragging himself gently through the close to his almshouse. I have seen Gloucester Cathedral sleeping, with a whole town sleeping with it. But if I want to think of a cathedral town I think, not of this, but of Barchester. Now even if I didn't happen to be a Civil Servant, a single visit to a post office would give me a more lively impression of the Public Service than all the volumes of *The Three Clerks* and *The Small House at Allington*. This seems to be a circumstance well worth noting, because this odd unreality manifests itself in nearly every other account of the Public Service that I have encountered. It seems almost as if there was something in the Public Service which refuses to be reduced to terms of life and art. Author after author rushes up to it determined to display its soul, and departs with a few melancholy strips of its outer garments. They begin one after another with the Civil Servant, and end with an ordinary man, who might just as well have been a soot-broker for all the effect his occupation has upon him. The explanation of this is not difficult to find. In order to describe anything vividly it is necessary to experience it at first hand. One of the distinctions, for example, between a good picture and a bad picture is that in the first case the painter sets down what he himself has actually seen, in the second the painter copies either what somebody else has seen, or, in many cases, failed to see. It is one of the most difficult feats in creation to throw away the deadening mists of use with which all objects of thought and sight are surrounded, and to see them fresh. In poetry, it would perhaps be true to say that we are only true poets in so far as we use words as Adam might have used them, with a little thrill of childish excitement. This is equally true of the author concerned with action and conduct. A great novelist strips off conventions and gets down to the simple facts behind them. But even he requires some assistance from the facts so revealed. The Civil Service gives little assistance. When the mummy wrapped in Red Tape is unswathed, what emerges is not a romantic Egyptian princess, but a stern and austere figure with something of Athene about her. For the art of Government does not fit easily into the ordinary human passion for vivid conflict. It is as hard to feel emotion about the correct decision as to the amount of unemployment benefit payable as to sob passionately because a flaw has been discovered in the Weber-Fechner law of reaction-times. It is difficult, but, as Mr. Wells has shown in his Utopias, not impossible. Even with Mr. Wells, his greatest successes in this form of fiction are achieved when he leaves Utopia and the Utopians, and concentrates with a sudden vivid grasp on something which is foreign

152

to both. In *Men Like Gods* the beautiful and slightly ridiculous ghosts hover faintly against the skyline of their lovely world, while Mr. Freddy Mush sticks out like a coster-monger at a Poetry Bookshop Reading. I hasten to add, in this connection, that I am not suggesting that Mr. Mush is a Civil Servant in fiction. On the contrary, I am satisfied that there never was, or could be, such a person, except in the creative mind of Mr. Wells. I conclude, therefore, on this that nobody has yet fallen in love with the Public Service as such. As a result we are presented either with the purely conventionalised Red Tape-worm, or, when the author is of sterner stuff, he loses his Civil Servant in the man. No great loss, some people would think.

This is what happens with Trollope. I take, because it is perhaps less known and because it is certainly a better book than *The Three Clerks, The Small House at Allington* to illustrate my point. The protagonists in this volume are Adolphus Crosbie of the General Committee Office and John Eames of the Income Tax Office. Comic relief is afforded by the figures, drawn with some little care, of Craddell, a sort of junior clerk in the Income Tax Office, and Sir Raffle Buffle, a Dickens Chairman of the Board, but with all the Dickens' punch left out. Adorning the fringes of the canvas, but not coloured in, are the faint shadows of Mr. Optimist, Major Fiasco, Mr. Kissing, and Mr. Love. (I may perhaps [in parenthesis] lose my temper and observe that anybody who was sufficiently lost to reason to invent such names deserves to be the hero of a Bloomsbury revival.) The story of the book is, even for Trollope, clumsy, conventional, and ridiculously untidy. There is a young woman, whose Christian name is Lily, and whose surname I have fortunately forgotten. She is wooed, won, and jilted by the swell, Adolphus Crosbie of the Whitehall Office, and is loved in vain and in silence (punctuated, however, as so often happens in these cases, by periodic and comparatively lengthy outcries) by John Eames, the hero. Mr. Crosbie, who is, for some reason unexplained, a figure in London Society, meets Lily when he has torn himself away from the General Committee Office to shoot with a friend. Adolphus, in spite of his determination to improve his position by marriage, so far forgets himself as to become affianced to Lily, who, though of respectable birth, has no money. She makes up for this, however, by being on the whole the silliest heroine in literature, and in consequence attracts equally the admiration of her author and the manly young Eames in the Income Tax Office. Mr. Crosbie leaves his affianced bride to stay at the castle of Lord de Courcy, and there permits himself to become engaged to one of the daughters of the house. The rest of the book, so far as the main story is concerned, is devoted to describing how Mr. Crosbie informed Lily of his change of mind, how Lily bore this news, how John Eames blacked Mr. Crosbie's eye at a railway station, how Mr. Crosbie married the

Earl's daughter, with deplorable results, and how in the end Lily and John didn't get married, because Trollope had made such a mess of describing Lily that he probably thought that his hero had better find a sweetheart for himself.

All this, in my view, is rubbish; but, as nearly always happens with Trollope, he imparts into the book something oddly real and sensible which is well worth reading and preserving. The good things in the book are the descriptions of the relations between John Eames and that very attractive nobleman the Earl de Guest. With great insight and fidelity Trollope has drawn an ordinary imperfect young man with all the natural likeableness of immature and blundering things, and a shrewd, decent English farmer, who is just enough of an aristocrat to have good manners. The other success is in the picture of silly Mr. Craddell and his amorous adventures in the boarding-house with Mrs. Lupex, the wife of a semi-drunken scene-painter. Trollope shows Craddell quite pointlessly fluttering round this rather musty candle, and the candle equally pointlessly singeing, while it gutters feebly, the moth's clumsy wings. There is no pretence and no violence in the picture. It is as inconclusive as Tchekov and as directly felt. It wasn't, perhaps, worth describing; it doesn't matter when it has been described. But if it is to be done at all, why, there it is; and it couldn't be bettered.

All of this, you will say, leaves out the Public

Service, even though Messrs. Crosbie, Eames, and Craddell all happen to be Public Servants. It does, but I warned you that it would be so. It is true that Trollope describes scenes in the Income Tax and the General Committee Offices, and dimly introduces a few additional officials. But he falls into the second class of authors, who, in coping with the Civil Service, realise that you'd better get on with life. It is plain that Trollope is always bored when he is representing Messrs. Kissing and Love quarrelling about posting the letter-book, and equally uninterested when describing the Board meeting of the General Committee Office. He suggests faintly that the clerks are wasting their time, and that the Members of the Board have nothing in particular to do. But he never even hints at the nature of the work performed by either. If Kipling had been doing it, he would have invented the work in such a way that nobody who did it could possibly recognise it, and nobody who read about it could fail to. But Trollope secretly believes that the work isn't worth doing at all, and therefore scurries off to love-making and taking, and the other real business of life. The only Civil Servant that he presents as such, and not as a human being, is the Sir Raffle Buffle, who makes his Private Secretary fetch his boots, and with him he fails completely. Sir Raffle Buffle doesn't exist at all, and, if he did, he would exist by virtue of the defects of snobbery and arrogance, which even Trollope must have known were not peculiar to the higher Public Officials. With a sigh of obvious relief Trollope plunges into John's ineffective wooing of Lily, into the amiable detail of quiet country life, and into the silly squalor of the boarding-house. The Public Service — that "mobled queen" — is left to wilt in limbo.

After Dickens and Trollope a great hush descends upon the Public Service. This is particularly odd, because in that period the Service was really suffering a dramatic change. If Dickens and Trollope are to be believed, it stood in their time for doing nothing at all. If modern writers are to be believed, the fault of the Public Service of to-day is that it attempts to do everything, everywhere, all the time. Mr. Tite Barnacle remains as adhesive as ever, but he is no longer content with the hull of the ship; he has somehow got himself stuck among the engines. Every time that the ship encounters heavy weather, or even strikes a rock, it is obvious that the fault lies with the now only too agile shellfish. Yet this momentous revolution completely escaped the notice of the later Victorian writers. Out of the wan lounger in offices, dimly reminiscent of a saloon-bar, begins slowly to develop the sinister shape of the Bureaucrat, and there is nobody found to warn Britain of her danger — at least, nobody that I have been able to discover.

I have considered George Eliot, Charlotte Brontë, Charles Reade of the earlier, and George Meredith and Thomas Hardy of the later, giants. I can find no trace of the Public Servant. Doctors, clergymen, architects, lawyers, soldiers, and sailors — all of them abound, but the Public Servant does not as much as cast a shadow in these august pages. It is true that Diana in *The Crossways* so far forgets herself as to marry "a gentlemanly official," but to the best of my knowledge, like a good Civil Servant, this person remains wrapped in anonymity. Thomas Hardy doesn't even go as far as that: there are, it would seem, not ten good Public Servants to be found in all Wessex.

I am, of course, prepared to be told that these statements are merely the result of inadequate reading, and that, in addition to Disraeli's *Endymion,* there are half a dozen books of first-rate importance in which a Public Servant and the Public Service play a leading part. Suppose, for example, some far better-read critic were suddenly to observe, " There is Thomas Carlyle." What could I say in reply except, " There is; only I haven't read him, and I don't intend to, not even (as seems improbable) if all his heroes are Public Servants." Carlyle, I might add, wrote some fifty or sixty longish volumes in praise of resolute silence, and therefore had no business (even if he did) to deal with the Public Servant, who spends almost as many years in the practice of it. But I expect that Thomas Carlyle shared Dr. Johnson's view of the Civil Servant as expressed in his dictionary definition of the Exciseman. And even if he didn't I would draw attention to the title of this

158

paper, which ought to have been " *Some* Public Servants in Fiction."

So that, having crossed the desert, we reach the works of our older contemporaries, from whom I select only H. G. Wells, E. V. Lucas, and Rudyard Kipling. Arnold Bennett I reserve for the post-war outburst of interest in what its professors believe to be the Public Service, but is, one is anxious to assert, something very different. Mr. Wells, as a professing Socialist, has naturally an interest in administration, but his Public Servant is, in that mood, not a picture of what exists, but of what should exist. When he remodels the world

nearer to the heart's desire

he does not contemplate a state of affairs where the existing Public Service has been extended, but where Private Service has ceased to exist. You may, of course, say that his solution is to make the whole population Public Servants, and that thus he has reached the very opposite pole from that to which Dickens nailed his flag. You might argue, since *Little Dorrit* is an argument for the abolition of the Public Service and *A Modern Utopia* is an argument for its universal expansion, that Mr. Wells is as enthusiastic a devotee of the Public Servant as Dickens a critic. That is in a sense true. Mr. Wells, in his Socialist mood, does believe in good administration as a remedy for the world's malady, and, what is more, sometimes actually appears to believe that it can be attained. But we should be congratulating ourselves too hastily if we assumed that it is anything in the Public Servant of to-day which inclines Mr. Wells to that roseate view. In his Socialist moments Mr. Wells believes that the State should definitely control all enterprise, and that private competition should be eliminated. But the dominant figure in the new world is to be a philosopher-ruler, whose philosophy is contained in what Kant might have called, " A Critique of Pure Science." Mr. Wells sweeps aside all the litter of capitalist and business civilisation, and increasingly clearly concentrates on a magic world where science and applied mathematics have taken control. This idea can be seen steadily growing in force throughout his writings, both sociological and romantic. It culminates in his last Utopia of *Men like Gods* where science has come to her own and, in a world perfectly ordered, human intelligence has addressed itself to the conquest of new dimensions. Nobody can read these visions without feeling the creative warmth of a profound mind, rotating with the easy force of a dynamo, and nobody, who is both young and intellectually eager, can resist holding out his hands to that attractive flame. But nobody could conceivably detect the faintest resemblance between the cold and austere figures of Mr. Wells's Valhalla of the Scientific Saints and the morning-coated, well-intentioned, but astoundingly pointless Civil Servant of Mr. Wells's actual acquaintance. For in *Ann Veronica* we are presented in

160

the person of Mr. Manning with a Civil Servant who, if painted in the colour of broad farce, would still seem to convey the view that Mr. Wells has of Public Servants. Mr. Manning is, several of the characters in the book assure us, a gentleman. This view is not borne out by anything in his conduct or conversation. He is further announced to be a comparatively successful Civil Servant. This is a regrettable declaration, because it would seem that success in the Civil Service is not incompatible with the intellectual equipment of a sentimental housemaid. Mr. Manning woos and (very temporarily) wins Ann Veronica by conventional outbursts in Capital Letters. But he does not stop at Capital Letters: he goes even further: he writes Verse, and he assures his lady, when she accepts him, that he proposes to burst into Mighty Lines. Mr. Wells gives us an example of these mighty lines. I do not quote them, but I think that it would be fair to say that in any other profession a person capable of their emission would be filing his petition. I may be wrong in supposing that Mr. Wells regards this pretentious donkey as in any way a typical Public Servant. But if I am, I can't help asking myself why, if he desired a foil for the scientist who was to win Ann Veronica, he should of all the professions have chosen a Civil Servant. The answer seems to be that Mr. Wells wanted the completest contrast that he could find to the life of adventure and romance, as typified in Ann Veronica and her biologist. He found the contrast ready-made by adopting the conventional view of the deadly dullness and unswerving fidelity to routine of the Public Servant.

This same point of view is sustained with all his gentle (and perhaps sometimes anæmic) charm by Mr. Lucas. Mr. Lucas is never harsh, and if he says " boo " to a goose, he makes it perfectly clear that that would be a very silly goose whose feelings would be ruffled by so tender an ejaculation. But if, as in the case of the Public Servant, he says boo to a swan, that less tractable fowl may have some cause for resentment. For nobody likes being mistaken, even in the tenderest way, for a goose, and I am afraid that there is no doubt that Mr. Ingleside — Mr. Lucas' charming Public Servant — is a most palpable goose. Of him, for example, Mr. Lucas observes that he held a high position in an office in Whitehall, but that his detractors suggested that Mr. Ingleside was in some doubt as to which the office was. That is a very gentle Lamb-like version of the Trafalgar Square fountains that play from ten to three. And throughout Mr. Ingleside is Mr. Manning conceived by our modern Lamb — without the mint sauce. Mr. Lucas does, in fact, see the Public Servant through the spectacles of India House, which may perhaps be described as tea-coloured. If he had thought of it first, Mr. Lucas would have made Mr. Ingleside excuse the lateness of his arrival at work on the score of the earliness of his departure. What is painful in all this, to one who thinks well of the Public Service, is that Mr. Lucas reflects in his polished way what a large number of very likeable and pleasant people think. It is, on the whole, rather more discouraging than the rather savage Wells caricature.

Then there is Mr. Kipling. It is perhaps unnecessary to say that the Public Servant who stays at home does not figure largely in Mr. Kipling's vision. Generally speaking, Mr. Kipling is unconscious of the existence of the middle classes, except when they go Overseas, in which case they become automatically aristocrats, and so worthy of notice. There are, of course, two Mr. Kiplings. The first is one of the most noticeable writers of short stories in the English language, and the author of five or six first-rate poems. The second Mr. Kipling is the English master of " The Hymn of Hate " school. The first Mr. Kipling is distinguished by an infinite capacity for loving. The second Mr. Kipling is equally distinguished by a capacity for hating. This hatred has not the large quality of his love: it is not steady, it is not profound, it is not permanent. It is ill-tempered, and ill-mannered. It bears to the frescoes in *Kim,* drawn and coloured with the loving care of an Italian master, the relation of a spiteful drawing on a wall by a schoolboy in a hurry.

Unhappily it is the second Mr. Kipling who has concerned himself with the Public Servant at home, while the first Mr. Kipling has paid some attention to the Public Servant abroad. There is a reference in a tale called *The Puzzler* to the home Civil Servant. That particular story deals with the amazing adroitness with which a Colonial Premier obtained audience of the leading Members of the Cabinet, upon a matter of first-class imperial importance, by the expedient of helping to capture a monkey that had climbed a monkey-puzzle tree. Mr. Kipling does not altogether approve of the fact that this is (apparently) the only way in which a Colonial Premier can obtain such an audience. He is indulgent, however, because the Cabinet Ministers in question are all members of the Upper Classes. But while both he and the Colonial Premier are (quite naturally) prepared to forgive the Cabinet Ministers on this ground, they are not prepared to treat the less amply born Public Servants in the same way. In response to the Colonial Premier's complaint of his treatment by a Public Official, Mr. Kipling observes, " I told him the story of the three-million pound insurrection caused by a deputy Under-Secretary sitting upon a mass of green-labelled correspondence instead of reading it." After that both he and the Colonial Premier feel themselves able to cope with the monkey.

The first Mr. Kipling, however, has very different things to say of the Overseas Public Servant. To him the Indian Civilian is one of the most sympathetic figures in modern life. His uniform strength and silence may become in the long run a little tedious, but in a story such as " At the End of the Passage," written in the language of the heart and not of the *Daily Mail,* Mr. Kipling presents a tragically vivid picture of men with infinite courage and endurance carrying the weight of Public Service under conditions unspeakably difficult. Allowing for the prejudices of the second Mr. Kipling, the first Mr. Kipling has, alone of all writers dealing with the Public Service, driven home the truth that this service may be as romantic as a crusade, as arduous as a pilgrimage, and as unrewarded as a martyrdom. Do not suppose that I am for a moment suggesting that this is a reasonable picture of the Public Service, even carried on at a distance, but it suggests to me that perhaps some day the first Mr. Kipling might (in the unlikely event of his meeting him) point out to the second Mr. Kipling that what is in India one of the highest of human aspirations need not necessarily decline in England to the least tolerable of imbecilities.

Before passing to the war and post-war novel of the Public Service, I should, perhaps, apologise for having omitted the Diplomatic Service from consideration. My reason for this omission is that the Diplomat is not, in eyes of writers of fiction, a Public Servant in the sense that I am using the phrase here. The complaint that one might be entitled to make against the portrayal of the normal Public Servant is that one feature of his life and activity is seized upon to the exclusion of all the others. In the case of the Diplomat the complaint rather is that the picture is based on nothing whatever. The ordinary Public Servant, it is grudgingly admitted, occasionally performs service, if very indifferent service, but the Diplomat never serves at all. He is either a young attaché who has incautiously strayed out of a novel by Ouida, and loses no time in returning thither at the earliest moment, or he is an ambassador, engaged in intrigues and plots so secret and so subtle that it is often only at the end of his career that he learns his own name. Diplomacy is thus roughly divided between attachés who are always known by nicknames and ambassadors who are concealed under numerals. Even when ambassadors are admitted into serious literature the fact that they are engaged in the romantic avocation of preventing or propagating wars removes from them the stigma of being associated with Public Service.

I can, therefore, with a comparatively easy mind, address myself to the post-war novel. I said in an earlier part of this paper that after Dickens and Trollope a great hush descended upon the Civil Service. During and after the war, on the other hand, a howling tempest raged through, round, and over it. The country was like a man suddenly attacked by indigestion. He never knew that he had a digestive system, and when he wakes up and discovers it he wishes that he hadn't. In the same way the country didn't know that it was being governed, as long as the Government was easy, sweet, and normal. When it became difficult, sour, and abnormal, the country thought that, on the whole, it would rather not be governed. Great Britain, in fact, awoke to the existence of its Public Service just about the time that it was disappearing to make way for the Business Men. " What I want," said the country after a painful pause,

" is not government, but business." " You shall have it," was the unanimous reply, and Great Britain got it.

Along with business, however, it got a large number of other things which it also deserved, and not least the novelists. The novelists had often heard of the Public Service, but they had the idea that it was something that Mr. Sidney Webb had invented, and, that being so, they hadn't read it. Now they were picked up by the scruff of the neck, and pitched into the middle of what must have seemed to them to be somebody else's dream. It had all the worst features of a dream. Things were happening in every direction, and with no apparent connection or purpose. Masses of paper, fabulously inscribed, billowed round them, generally labelled " Urgent," and remained in the same place for months. Men in top hats, smoking cigars, stamped up and down corridors, led by boy-scouts to the most unexpected encounters. Women swept in and out of rooms with the baffled air of participators in a Bargain Sale who had found their way into a church. Soldiers — red-tabbed and brass-hatted — passed in platoons, engaged upon urgent military enterprises; and members of the public in large numbers, who had come to ask questions, remained to sign the form which enrolled them as officers of the Department. In the middle of all of this, a few — a very few — of the entirely discredited remnants of the old Civil Service sat, learning (as it seemed to the novelists) that what is required to cope with a war is not Red Tape but Blue Ruin.

The novelists may be forgiven if they gathered a mistaken impression, in these circumstances, of what the Public Service is. They may also be excused if many of them sought refuge from it in the comparative quiet of the trenches. Nor is it surprising that those who remained should almost unanimously have decided that the only way to keep their mental balance was to describe what they saw and heard.

The result from the point of view of the present paper is two-fold. In the first place it is a most unfortunate circumstance that, when this unrivalled opportunity of describing the Public Servant in fiction presented itself, there were practically no Public Servants left to describe. In the next place, there is a most embarrassing wealth of material. There is hardly a novel of the period that does not introduce its Public Servants. That was inevitable, since the population was roughly divided into those who fought the enemy abroad and those who fought one another at home. Even if I confine myself to novels devoted solely to Government Departments I am confronted with a baker's dozen. In these circumstances I shall choose one novel only, *The Old Indispensables,* chiefly because, alone of all the novels, it has occupied itself, not only with the war kaleidoscope, but also in a very intimate and penetrating way with a few real Public Servants. It is with regret that I deny myself the opportunity of beginning with Miss Rose Macaulay's *What Not* and Mrs. Blanco-White's *Give and Take.* Miss· Macaulay's book, however, is frankly farcical, dealing as it does with the antics of the Ministry of Brains. It abounds, as anything Miss Macaulay writes must, in sudden brilliant flashes where mere wit dissolves into profound understanding. It has also more than its share of absolutely first-rate jokes, as when the War Cabinet is described as " Five minds with but a single thought — if that," or in the numerous and always enchanting announcements of the Safety-if-possible Council. But Miss Macaulay does not pretend to give a picture of the Public Servant in fiction. She is drawing the *reductio,* not only *ad absurdum,* but *ad diabolum,* of all the worst tendencies that the war imposed upon public administration. Mrs. Blanco-White's book, on the other hand, is a most faithful analysis of war administration. She has taken a Blue Book and converted it into a Yellow Book. But living, formidable, and complete as the book is, it still does not deal with the regular Public Servant. It is a record of the great encroaching sea of business, and only an occasional bubble on the surface indicates the faint attempt of some submerged Public Servant to breathe. It is with equal regret that I abstain from following Mr. Bennett and Mr. Prohack in their Golden Journey to that perfect symbol of unutterable wealth — the £30,000 Yacht. I confess that I, like Mr. Bennett, would prefer to put the Treasury behind me, and, acquiring a quarter of a million sterling, would like to know what it feels like to have a Turkish bath because you don't need one, and to be able to order ties by the furlong and shirts by the acre. But alas! my subject is Public Servants in Fiction, not in Fairyland. I must, therefore, abandoning Mr. Prohack to enjoy the astonishments of wealth and its expenditure with a mind elaborately equipped with the mechanism for such surprise by twenty years spent in the Treasury, return to Mr. Edward Shanks and *The Old Indispensables*. Mr. Shanks, alone of those who have reduced Civil Servants to fiction, has been interested at first hand in the effect upon actual persons of conditions (even if abnormal conditions) in a Government Office. Mr. Shanks takes nothing for granted. He does not assume that a bureaucrat is a traditional figure reacting to traditional impulses. He does not regard the Civil Service as a curse or a blessing. He neither admires nor despises public administration. Fate presented this unusually sensitive (and expressive) mind with a perfect godsend in the form of a complete and entirely new little world, living at fever heat under the burning glass of war. He jumps into it like a schoolboy with a bright half-crown in his pocket storming a tuck-shop. " Golly! " he says.

The result is that not only do his Public Servants live, but he has given a perfectly consistent picture of the Civil Servant during the war as seen through the eyes of an intelligent, able, forbearing, and altogether likeable Staff Clerk. He does what Trollope was too little interested, and Dickens too uninformed, to do. He considers what happens in the Civil Service seriously as something happening in the mind of his Civil Serv-

170

ants, and, though he indulges more than once in touches of farce, it is perfectly and (indeed to a Civil Servant) painfully probable farce. His hero is Mr. Evans, that inimitable roarer down telephones, who, with his friend Mr. Roper — also a Staff Clerk — remains in the mind with the little happy glow with which one remembers a rather jolly friend or a rather jolly moment. Mr. Evans, in a world where everybody is generally wrong and rather proud of it, is almost invariably right and takes it for granted. He is conscientious, wideawake, genial, and kindly. It is true that he has rather less conscience than he should have about the disposal of files, and is perhaps a little too interested in baked jam-roll. But, files, baked jam-roll, and a tendency to correct a draft containing " communication " by inserting " letter " and one containing " letter " by inserting " communication," and all, he is the salt of the earth.

And just as the Civil Service is shown as a part of Mr. Evans, so it is shown as a part of all the official hierarchy, Mr. Pyeblew and Mr. Harper, the eagerly aspiring Upper Division juniors, Mr. Barnet, the Assistant Director, who was probably born an Assistant Director and will certainly die one, and the smooth, easy, intriguing Director, whose Christian name was obviously designed by Providence to support a title. All of them, not forgetting their secretaries and the Minister's secretaries, live by virtue of their reactions on their work, so that when you think of any of them you see their environment with them.

The actual story is not of first-rate importance. It is enough to say that it concerns the struggles of a Contracting Department during the war to maintain itself against the assaults of all other Departments, against the public, against the inevitable outside Committee of Inspection, and against itself. Mr. Evans in due course reaps his reward in a £600 post, Mr. Pyeblew succeeds in christening himself Controller of Tombstones, Mr. Harper declines to the charge of the Registry of the Tramways Office, Mr. Barnet missed the C.B., so obviously his due, owing to the fact that, when his Permanent Secretary was putting his name forward for that merited decoration, he had dictated, " I therefore put his name forward for the C.B. He — " and then his mind wandered. The typist dropped the aspirate, and Mr. Barnet found himself a Commander of the Order of the British Empire. Finally Sir William Blood defeated his Inspection Committee. But all this matters very little. What does matter is that one book without malice or praise has honestly and imaginatively set down one glimpse of the Public Service as it was.

I began by quoting Milton's line:

They also serve who only stand and wait.

You will see that the general view appears to be that what Public Servants serve is generally a double fault. But somehow they don't lose the set.

MODERNISM IN VERSE

Modernism In Verse

In an earlier dialogue I had sought for a definition of poetry, and, after a long and perhaps unconvincing pursuit, had reached the rather plebeian conclusion that " verse is the expression with authority of what is significant in life by means of the fusion of thought and sound." You may suppose that, though I tested that definition by applying it to a number of contemporary reputations, I did not feel that I had really done justice to the Modernist school of thought. All my conclusions were directly opposed to theirs, and I had no reason to imagine that either in practice or precept they were not at least equally likely to be right as myself. That being so, I turned back to their verse, as illustrated in Great Britain by the Sitwells and Herbert Read, in the United States by T. S. Eliot, Conrad Aitken, John Gould Fletcher, and Archibald Macleish. Unhappily, the more I read of them the more convinced I became that their successes and failures equally proved my theory rather than theirs. I asked Harold Bypass, therefore, to deliver a lecture to me, promising only to interrupt for the sake of obtaining information, but adding, of course, that after he had concluded I should indicate what difficulties, if any, he had failed to solve.

We dined at Jack Straw's Castle, and after dinner on an unexpectedly mild June evening we walked along the Spaniards, and sat at the edge of the Heath watching the evening invest London with the fugitive similitude of Petra. Well, I said, Bypass, when I last spoke of these matters it was with R. and Delarue at St. Cergue, and there, too, " the enchantress " played her misleading tunes to some purpose. Mont Blanc, whether in the full livery of day or in the cooler costume of night, would not let us be. I think, in fact, the Mountain entirely confused Mahomet by coming to him, with the result that Delarue and the theories of Modernist verse were lost in a snowdrift. I heard something of that, said Bypass, and R. tells me that you behaved with more than your usual shamelessness. It seems that you poured rhetoric over Delarue — like slops poured out of a high window in an Italian hill-city on a surprised pedestrian. Delarue emerged drenched and angry, and your defence apparently was that you had only been clearing your own mind and hadn't noticed the traffic below. I warn you, however, that I have an umbrella. Yes, I said, Delarue was cross, and I do feel that I spoiled the argument by dithyrambs. But the trouble about verse is that it is so infectious. I assure you that for more than three hours I was a mirror of all that was dull and prosaic, but when I found that my attitude was being taken for granted as a confession of

176

defeat, I did rather overflow the banks. I've told you that I shan't repeat the offence, or at any rate not till you have more than had your turn.

Well, said Bypass, on that understanding I will advance one or two points, though I know perfectly well that you regard yourself as Socrates confronted by a not unamiable sophist. Nonsense, Bypass, I said, if we are to have comparisons, compare me rather to entirely innocent Rosa Dartle with never a suspicion of a godlike Steerforth. My dear Humbert, he replied, you may perhaps with justice envisage yourself as a character out of one of the more sentimental passages of Dickens, but for my part I remain a quiet figure of real life in the post-war year 1928. I do not propose to embark on seduction nor, let me tell you, to suffer it. Very well, I said, let all that is mid-Victorian and second-rate in me listen across half-a-century to the stripped athletic mind of to-day, confessing, as I once ventured to observe in a verse of Tennyson,

> *I did not shrink from thought. I understood,*
> *although industrialism is the devil,*
> *(God save our gracious Queen!) that somehow good*
> *is always somehow evil.*

May I remind you, said Bypass, that you had asked me to explain the principles of Modernist verse to you, but that so far more than half the time has been occupied by your not wholly relevant outbursts of facetiousness. Proceed, Bypass, I said.

Tu l'as bien dit, mais tu l'as trop bien dit.

Very well, said Bypass, I will, but you are to keep your word. It has been supposed, he went on, by fools or by those deliberately trying to confuse the issue, that the Modernist movement that we find in all the arts is a post-war product. Nothing could, of course, be less true. In painting, the Post-Impressionists had yielded to Gauguin, in sculpture Rodin was saluting Epstein from his mountain-peak, in prose Romain Rolland was on one end of the rope the middle of which was tied round Proust, and the end of which was just being grasped by the author of *The Dubliners,* and in verse Verlaine and Rimbaud had cleared the way for imagists, who were *malgré eux* the forerunners of T. S. Eliot and the glories of Transatlantis regained. I make this digression into the obvious because it is so often pretended that in the last four or five years a wholly new and undigested view of Art has been thrust upon the world. Its defenders are accused of locking the stable door before Pegasus has arrived, or rather of locking it on a wooden hobby-horse, upon which they ride themselves in the childish belief that they are galloping to a distant and starry goal. That accusation is the product either of malice or ignorance. The truth is that we are now only trying to formulate the theory upon which all that is serious in Art has been acting in the last thirty or forty years.

Let me therefore begin by considering the point to

178

which Victorian Art had brought us in England, limiting myself for this purpose to prose and verse. There is at the moment a reaction in favour of Dickens and Tennyson, not because we think any better of them, but because we need no longer fear their influence. The dead hand has lost its grip, and we can regard them as dispassionately as the Elizabethans. If we can ascribe a principle to what was so obviously based on none, we should be entitled, I think, to say that Victorian Art aimed at " imitation of life," and that Matthew Arnold was merely crystallising what he saw to be current practice when he advanced that as the formula governing verse. The emphasis, however, is on " imitation " rather than on " life." Dickens, Art's eternal barnstormer, imitated life in a series of long-drawn-out, though sometimes brilliantly funny, charades. But to life as the realists understand it, life disposing of itself without screen or aid, he deliberately closed his mind. If, for example, he saw the grinding daily oppressions of the Poor Law system, he did not permit them in slow unemphatic and quietly abominable detail to express themselves. He dressed them for the fancy-dress ball, to which real characters are denied admittance, as Bumble — a grotesque denial by virtue of its unreality of the slow, cold realities it travestied. It is admitted that any artist must select, but Dickens selected like a photographer who, in adjusting his negative, either blurs all the outlines and leaves only the wrinkles, or for pathos omits everything but two large and unrelated eyes. Wandering, as he was thus compelled to, in a No Man's Land between the hostile trenches of unembellished fact and unembarrassed fancy, there was no reason why any story should ever stop. And it rarely ever did. But it must be observed that it is absurd to criticise him for his digressions. Life is, of course, a series of digressions. Dickens, like all the Victorians, is to blame, not for digressing, but for not having digressed all the time. What he sought to do, in fact, was to erect a series of signposts indicating fixed points round which the flux of events was to swirl. His Sairey Gamps, his Mr. Micawbers, his Mark Tapleys, haunt the grey persistent monotonies of reality, like highly-coloured ghosts suddenly appearing from time to time in a fog. Indeed, his art may be compared to that of a man on a station-platform trying to clean the windows of a train going through at sixty miles an hour. It is magnificent, but it is not window-cleaning.

MYSELF: I promised not to interrupt, but I should like to enquire, if life is an express-train, and if the windows are dirty, how they are to be cleaned by the artist who is *ex hypothesi* a spectator and not a passenger.

BYPASS: Window-cleaning is not the business of the artist. At any rate I think that I have indicated what our quarrel is with that approach to creation. Life must be permitted the maximum of independence, and should as far as possible go without having anything said for it. It may perhaps be objected that Dickens is an unfair choice from that point of view, and that a better test would have been afforded by Trollope. But Trollope is only Jane Austen reduced to a sort of powder, from which cup after cup of some tasteless fluid is distilled. It is the exact opposite of the truth to allege that what Trollope imitated was life. What he imitated was Jane Austen's refusal to recognise life. It is possible to refuse life and be a great artist. It is not possible to be one when you regard the act of refusal as a proof of acceptance.

Let me, however, turn from the novelists to Tennyson. When I think of him in his later periods I think always of his practice of going about with a note-book, in which he entered suitable epithets for subsequent use. It does not matter if the story is apocryphal; to revise the Italian witticism : *se non e ben trovato, e vero.* For a very short period, till he was about thirty-five, Tennyson permitted life to express itself in the form of bird-song. It cannot be denied that birds sing, nor that their singing, if undisturbed, has value. It celebrates in general the ecstasies of approaching wedlock, and is therefore a natural mode in which love disengages itself. We find, therefore, in *The Lady of Shalott* or *Mariana in the Moated Grange* no interference with the natural processes, and the result, therefore, is poetry as we can understand it. But after that period Tennyson began to take out his note-book and, looking about him, record life like a policeman taking down the facts of a collision.

He is, as it were, always prepared to give evidence to a possibly hostile court. But, unlike the policeman, he is permitted to disobey the rules of evidence. Not only what life said, but what it didn't say, and couldn't possibly have said, is admissible. Indeed Tennyson had now deliberately reached a point where he regarded life as suspiciously loitering, and liable to arrest in order to undergo the reformatory of the poet's mind. The perfect example of this process of devitalising and disinfecting reality is presented in *The Idylls of the King*. Sir Thomas Malory, in a hearty, bludgeoning sort of way, had stunned and isolated a number of reasonably romantic figures and episodes. The old man had, while assaulting them, still permitted them to stumble out their own dying speeches, and had not concealed the fact that, while the best art does not imitate the hero's dying noises, it does not, on the other hand, convert them into a Valentine. Arthur and Lancelot were, at least in the *Morte d'Arthur,* capable of death, if only because, unlike de Musset's beautiful lady, they had at least lived. But Arthur's Round Table served no purpose but that of rapping for spirits, who, true to the tradition of the medium, when evoked always spoke in Tennyson's undiluted idiom. Faintly the mailèd ghosts creaked and gibbered, deodorised, disappointed, and unhouseled. British verse at that moment had attained a point of unreality which inevitably demanded either extinction or the sharpest possible reaction.

MYSELF: Let me be clear, Bypass. The subject of your lecture, as I gather, is Modernism in verse. Up to the present moment you have contributed to that topic an attack on Charles Dickens for insufficient digression, on Trollope for having insisted on not being Jane Austen, and on Tennyson for having " died " at thirty-five. These in themselves are all important, though perhaps, in certain circles, disputable, propositions, but for the moment their exact bearing escapes me. For example, if I may take Tennyson, do I understand that he is the unwilling creator of modern verse, insisting on making it not in his own image? Because, if that is so, I shall expect you to reinforce your spirited abuse by indicating in what particulars he offends. Is it only his mind that is at fault, or is his method equally wrong? Is his superb technique actually a flaw? Is his enrichment of lyrical language itself a crime? I should like especially to know what are the glaring defects of one of his later poems, *The Eagle*.

BYPASS: *The Eagle*. Did Tennyson write a poem called *The Eagle?*

MYSELF: Even the fact that you haven't read it doesn't disprove its existence. Let me, on the contrary, quote it:

> *He clasps the crag with crookèd hands*
> *Close to the sun in lonely lands,*
> *Ring'd with the azure world, he stands.*

The wrinkled sea beneath him crawls:
He watches from his mountain walls,
And like a thunderbolt he falls

"Crookèd hands" and "wrinkled sea" are good, I think, and I seem here to detect our poet, not so much imitating life, as proleptically imitating Miss Edith Sitwell.

BYPASS: I have not denied that, before he started thinking, Tennyson was a poet. Our objection to him is in his long-sustained rôle of the recorder of "The Confessions of a Second-rate Mind." I am surprised, however, that he should have written so good a poem in his declining years.

MYSELF: Perhaps declining years is a little excessive. The poem was published in 1851, when Tennyson was forty-two, an advanced but perhaps a not senile age. But I desire to call your attention to the fact that even after attaining that great age he had enough poetic vigour left to change the "hookèd hands" of the first edition to the perfect felicity of "crookèd" in a later edition. That will require some explanation.

BYPASS: Which I do not propose to give. I shall deal in a moment with the Tennysonian form, and will attempt to answer your specific questions then. I am here indicating what were the influences in Victorianism

184

which it was necessary rudely to disturb before Art could find itself again.

MYSELF: Perhaps, however, it would be convenient to dispose of Browning before you reach the release from mediocrity initiated in the 'nineties by Ernest Dowson and the Rhymers' Club.

BYPASS: In some ways we find Browning even a more deleterious influence than that of Tennyson. Tennyson at least admitted his invincible sentimentality. Browning for ever cloaked his essential simper with a rugged frown. Like Tennyson, he did in fact wear his heart on his sleeve, but he always pretended either that it wasn't a heart at all, but a mind, or, alternatively, that it was somebody else's. It is not open to dispute that intellectually he was immeasurably Tennyson's superior. But he was for ever obtruding his mind between the reader and the object of thought. It is possible, of course, to defend, even to admire, unswerving intellectualism, such as that of Mallarmé. But if the thought, as with Browning, has always an emotional tinge, reality is betrayed at every turn. It is the critical custom particularly to applaud Browning's *Men and Women* on the score of their large humanity. *Fra Lippo Lippi, Rabbi Ben Ezra,* and a hundred others, it is claimed, are the raw material of life, with just the little twist that lends the shape of immortality. It is, I admit, easy to be ensnared, and to suffer seduction, by the fragments of song in *Fra Lippo,* to feel a cold hand on the heart

185

when Childe Rolande winds the slug-horn, to sit in quiet wonder while a voice slowly and gravely murmurs:

Beautiful Evelyn Hope is dead,

or, above all, almost to feel round one's own neck the loop of hair that strangled Porphyria. But we must resist that impulse, and confess that this is virtuosity and not reality. This is not the stuff of life, but of books. Browning, like Thackeray, is not content to let his creatures be. He is for ever exhibiting them like a showman, or like an adroit theatrical producer. Take a story by Tchechov and set it beside *Fra Lippo,* and you have life confronting a theatrical representation.

MYSELF: It is odd, isn't it, that the Russians are so successful with life. Perhaps the explanation is partly that, having so much less of it than the rest of us, they treat it with more respect. I readily admit, of course, that Tchechov rather leaves life to its own devices. But it sometimes seems to me that it could have done with a little assistance.

BYPASS: Precisely, and that, I imagine, was Browning's view also. But I think that a more reasonable attitude would be to assume that life is quite capable of looking after itself without the help of those who participate in its indulgences. But what I have already said is not the most damaging part of our complaint against this poet. Our real accusation is that he gave the impression in his

186

earlier work, notably in *Sordello,* of having anticipated our conclusion that language, like life, must be left to speak for itself. We are entitled to assume that a national tongue in the process of time has become a living organism which directly crystallises and reacts to the life by which it is engendered. If, therefore, life must be allowed to have its way, the same attitude must be permitted to language. The poet's business is to suggest directions both to life and language, not arbitrarily to impose barriers or shapes. If he does, one thing or another is bound to happen. If the poet is actually in touch with life, then it will burst the barriers and destroy all his artificial groynes and embankments. It will flow shapeless, enormous, and vital, as it did, for example, with Blake when, as it constantly did, the tides of verse bolted, like a whole caravanserai of frightened horses.

Or if the writer is not a real poet, then life will be strangled, and we shall be presented with a series of empty coffins, beautifully caparisoned or roughly finished, according to the technical skill of the craftsman. In *Sordello,* as I said, it seemed as though Browning had decided to let words shift for themselves. But in his later work it became apparent that he was concealing his adhesion to the conventional view under a foam of irregular words, as a quiet sea may, under the impulse of some flaw of wind, suddenly toss a casual armful of spindrift in the eyes of a shore-watcher. After a time his very ruggedness became as conventional a mould as the sweetest Tennysonian lisp, and from time to time, throwing off all concealment, he could write verse as deliberately made as the invocation to *The Ring and the Book:*

> *O lyric love, half angel and half bird,*
> *And all a wonder and a wild desire.*

There you see Browning, the self-admitted romantic, hugging the words, not for their own sake, but for some inherently irrelevant association. He called them like spirits from the vasty deep, and, when they came in their dark beauty and obscurity, he gulped them down with a mouthful of soda. That, in our view, is a supreme betrayal both of life and verse, which should be life made manifest.

MYSELF: You find this poor Browning, then, like Clara Middleton, going about " with a romantic tale hanging from her eyelashes." But is then, romance, as such, inadmissible in verse? And if so, what is romance? Is it the opposite of classicism? or is it not a mode at all, but merely an outbreak? Or do you go further and say that the so-called " classics " are merely the romantics with a pinch of salt on their fairy-tales? Are you, in a word, suggesting, as you know you are accused of suggesting, that the first poem in the English language was written when T. S. Eliot composed *Waste-Land?*

BYPASS: We are maintaining nothing of the sort. We naturally believe in progressive development in verse as in everything else. We do not expect Homer to write like Sophocles, nor Shakespeare like E. E. Cummings.

MYSELF: You will forgive me if I interrupt to applaud your concession to Shakespeare. I should, I confess, have been sorry to have had to jettison William.

BYPASS: Do not worry, my dear Humbert. The only windmills against which we are tilting are made of papier-maché, or, more precisely, of waste-paper. They may smother us as they collapse by mere weight, but, believe me, they will collapse. I repeat that verse must adjust itself to the changes in life itself. A " Romaunt de Rolland " has a genuine significance when life is a battle in armour between Christian and Saracen, when a slug-horn may actually be blown across forlorn mountains, carrying in its last high note the downfall of a period of the world. Or you may write a *Henry V* when fighting is a keen individual encounter between caravel and high-pooped galleon under the dusty winds of an earlier world. Life is animal, life is jocund, and to portray it like a novel by Joyce would in that period be criminal. Indeed, if D. H. Lawrence had written *Women in Love* in the sixteenth century, he would have been guilty of romanticism.

MYSELF: I am beginning to understand. There is for you neither romantic nor classic, but only life set free. The true performer in each age is he who provides the deepest channel for those raging waters. Do you, however, maintain that nothing in the Victorian Age corresponded, and gave an outlet, to contemporary life? Must we abandon, not only Tennyson and Browning, but must the author of *The Scholar-Gipsy* and *The Forsaken Merman* be deserted on a littered beach, long forsaken by the racing tides? Because if you maintain this point of view about Browning and Matthew Arnold, I shall be driven to believe that you mean by life not anybody's life, but a curiously limited life, of the kind that is peculiar to a disillusioned post-war generation. I begin to fear that you do not merely excommunicate rival points of view, but like the Red Queen in *Alice,* you insist on their immediate execution. I suspect that your real accusation against Browning is not that he denied life, but that he denied your kind of life. Browning, like Walt Whitman, whom he so closely resembled in spirit, held out both arms to life, and almost strangled her in a gorilla embrace. But the life he knew and welcomed returned the embrace eagerly. She was a great lazy woman — like one of the bishop's smooth, marble-limbed mistresses. She was a Gioconda, with a smile painted in by Hogarth, but eyes darkened with all the pains of Juliet and Cordelia. And, with all that, she walked

> *breast-forward,*
> *Never doubting clouds would break.*

You may not like her. She might be embarrassing at a Bloomsbury reception. But you could no more deny her life than you could to a tiger crouching for the spring. And as for Matthew Arnold, he did actually stand between two ages,

One dead, one powerless to be born,

and the conflicts and indecisions of the dead and the unliving do pine with bat-voices in a heart-breaking undertone through all his verse. Do you blame him because he subdued that restlessness and anguish to the perfection of tranquil victory, as in the end of *Sohrab and Rustum*. Because "the majestic river" which there floats on out of the hum and mist of that "low land" is the very river of life of which you speak, leaving the heights for the parcelled and dusty plains on its long voyage to the looked-for home of waters beyond the world.

BYPASS: My dear Humbert, I know you too well to lose my temper with you. Delarue, I understand, stamped off into the pines. I shall not fly angrily between the bushes of the Lower Heath, leaving you to address even more pompous soliloquies of verse triumphant to the lights of London. No! it grows cold, and, as a penalty for having scandalously interrupted, you will pay for a taxi to Tavistock Square. We will there, on my ground, renew the argument, when you are no longer assisted by the adventitious arguments of so candle-clear a moon.

Very well, I said, Bypass, I will provide the taxi, but at least admit that the moon — a natural object after all — seems not unsympathetic to my point of view.

If you continue in that strain, said Bypass, you will drive me to remind you of the derivation of the word lunatic.

I was saying, said Bypass, settling down into an armchair, before you burst in with your Italian city trick, foiled on this occasion by the umbrella of which I warned you, that we did not deny that life varied its courses, and therefore its manifestations, throughout the centuries. It by no means follows, if the original verse-form invented is sufficiently elastic, that it will not meet the need for a considerable period. But the time must come, and indeed always does come, when the old form definitely becomes inappropriate. Thereafter it must be immediately discarded and a new one provided. I will not insult your slight acquaintance with the history of verse by pointing out how the Greeks successively discarded the epic for the lyrical and dramatic, the hexameter for the iambic. That is a commonplace of poetic history. But, like all commonplaces, it has its heroes and its martyrs as it has its tyrants and its persecutors.

MYSELF: And I, my dear Bypass, though enjoying your hospitality, am preparing your *auto-da-fé?*

192

BYPASS: If you could, my poor Humbert; but what you, like the reactionaries of every period, are attempting to do, is not to set back the clock, but to deny the existence of Time. That is what Tennyson did. By 1830, or at latest 1842, he had said all that life had to say to and through him. It was, as I said earlier, a whispering bird-life, light breath in green branches, and here and there the flash of an arrow-like wing. Listen!

> *She only said, " My life is dreary,*
> *He cometh not," she said.*
> *She said, " I am aweary, aweary,*
> *I would that I were dead."*

That is a gentle beauty of life between the leaves, a little marred by being seen in the looking-glass of Keats, but still life choosing the pretty tricks appropriate to her gentle graces. But that, of course, could not last. Everybody who is a poet begins with the bird-note. The test begins when the birds are quiet. It is then that the deep stirrings of the earth are heard, low, mutinous, and obscure. The test of the poet and of poetry is whether that everlasting enigma can attain the transitory solution for which it unceasingly strives. How does Tennyson respond to that test? From the moment that the birds were quiet, the world became for him a menacing blank. He was alone in Sahara where there is no wind. It was so still that he could hear his own mind stir in the scorching sand like a crumpled leaf. He did not do the only honest thing, which was to admit that life, and therefore poetry, had done with him. Life had dictated a technique to the young lover. The middle-aged politician of verse sought to ensnare the non-existent in those rusting cages. The result was disastrous. Not only did Tennyson himself write volume after volume of entirely useless verse, but, because he remained technically supreme, he dominated the world of English poetry for nearly half a century. Tennyson all his life was haunted by his father's ghost, the child being father to the man. Sepulchrally it muttered the secrets of the prison-house, in which that lost boy who had adored Keats was confined. With deeper and deeper notes it intoned *The Charge of the Light Brigade, Welcome to Alexandra, Ode on the Duke of Wellington*. There came a time when criticism overhearing the subterranean grumbles of *The Northern Farmer,* might well have cried with Hamlet:

> *Well said, old mole!*
> *Canst move in the earth so fast?*

And all this time contemporary poets drowned slowly in the stagnant pool of Tennysonian prettiness. Browning, it is true, appeared to revolt, but, as I have already said, he had only turned Tennyson's singing-robes inside out, showing the shaggy lining. The material of which they were woven was the same in both cases. This being the state of affairs, either poetry was dead, or something violent was bound to happen. Matthew Arnold, I am prepared to admit, initiated a faint struggle against the predominating influence. But, like *The Scholar Gipsy,* he early fled

our greetings, fled our tears and smiles.

There was nothing except a tired old man laboriously playing Romeo on an empty stage to a long-forgotten Juliet. But there was a hand on the curtain.

MYSELF: And was the hand Swinburne's or Ernest Dowson's? Was life rallying its forces in the person of that bright young Satyr, or in the whispered addresses of the pale Pierrot of a Minute?

BYPASS: Neither one nor the other. Swinburne does not belong to the history of English poetry. He is a flame at the side of the road, or perhaps even a wandering, though beautiful will-o'-the-wisp. In a sense, of course, Swinburne is a reaction against the mild lowings of the later Tennysonian period. That period reached its public consummation when Tennyson was good enough to inquire of his sovereign if her duties gave her time to read a trifle which so inconsiderable a thing as the first poet of the age had tossed off. Yes, said Lord Tennyson,

Her court was pure: her life serene;
God gave her peace: her land reposed.

"Her land reposed?" Swinburne, no doubt, felt that it was snoring, and he proceeded with a certain shrill violence to wake it up. His violence was justified, and was not wholly unsuccessful. But the truth was that

Swinburne was reacting against the superficial and not the fundamental evils of the age. He saw a period wrapped in a greasy cloak of self-satisfaction and maudlin comfort, a period in which Christianity was broadening down " from precedent to precedent " till it had become entirely featureless, a period when in public the existence of the body was, if not denied, at least questioned. Swinburne jumped into the ring crying " Aphrodite! " and sent blow after blow at the heavy swollen face of his antagonist.

> *What ailed us, O gods, to desert you*
> *For creeds that refuse and restrain?*
> *Come down and redeem us from virtue,*
> *Our lady of Pain.*

Naturally the world-weary Titan resented the small impact of this rose-loaded fist. But Swinburne had not learned the art of the body-blow. He took over his ring-craft from his adversaries, and boxed lightly by the rules that Tennyson had invented. He proclaimed himself a pagan, but he was, in fact, a true believer in the old poetic creed. He saw that contemporary thought was false and smug, but he did not realise that it could not be defeated on the ground that it had itself chosen. Wilder and wilder became his protest, and sweeter and more conventional the form in which it was uttered, till in the plays there was little to choose between him and the author of " Thomas à Beckitt." Swinburne was in emotional, but not in intellectual, opposition to his age. Life used his heart, while it was still malleable, but it never had access to his mind. The result was that Swinburne's influence in the long run was almost identical with that of Tennyson, in that it betrayed his followers by the artificial beauty of form, and did not lead them along the path of stern intellectual refusal to be doped by the philosophic fraud of a pea-green period, universally suffering from the Bright's disease propagated from Birmingham. Swinburne blazed up and out. His is perhaps an abiding light for youth, but his torch changed nothing and changes nothing.

MYSELF: And Dowson?

BYPASS: You are, of course, not serious. *The 'Nineties* was a second-rate poem written in a moment of self-contempt by de Musset. Swinburne, I said, did not belong to the history of English poetry. *The 'Nineties* does not belong to any history at all. Professor Garrod's translation of the last verse of *La Mort* disposes of the time when Oscar Wilde and Aubrey Beardsley used the yellow streak in their artistic consciousness to dye the book which is the chief memorial of a non-existent decade:

> *She never lived; but drops, being dead,*
> *This make-belief of life, this look*
> *Of living — letting fall the book*
> *She counterfeited to have read.*

MYSELF: And then?

BYPASS: Then we had the Boer War, and for a time the poet's aim was, if possible, to be generally accepted as " An absent-minded beggar." Kipling sang all out in dithyrambs of imperial fortitude that may perhaps be summed up in two verses as follows:

Revere this simple maxim:
That he who will not fight,
The other fellow smacks him,
And serve him damn well right.

Since though for meek and lowly
There is a place, the place is
(The Master tells us) wholly
Reserved for subject races.

This was, however, Chanticleer crowing to salute the dawn, which he believed that his shrill outcries engendered, but in which, in fact, he had no part.

MYSELF: And the dawn came with de la Mare, Yeats, Ralph Hodgson, James Stephens, Masefield, Rupert Brooke, and Flecker? Not, one would feel, too bad a conflagration in the East.

BYPASS: Yes and no. All these poets — and at least two, de la Mare and Hodgson, may be admitted to be real poets — played their part. But they could be described as a rescue-party, attempting the impossible task of reclaiming the lost tradition, rather than the pioneers making smooth the way for the Lord of the World. I will not stay to discuss their virtues and their failings. Each of them had some touch of elemental fire, which, laid on the right altar, might have blazed to Heaven. But each ultimately founders because he is sacrificing to the broken image of a dead god. For the priests we must look elsewhere.

MYSELF: Before you exhibit the Sacred College will you let me say that I think we have now reached the crucial point of difference between the Modernist and what I will call the Static before you label it the effete. Our argument would be that each of these poets has in his own way proved that there is nothing in the old forms, if a new mind is brought to them which conflicts with the expression of contemporary life in poetry. De la Mare and Yeats in particular have written in superficially traditional forms verse as ringingly fresh as Catullus. It is possible that they have no kinship with Mr. E. E. Cummings, Miss Marianne Moore, and Mr. Crow Ransom. But it is at least possible to argue that the reason of that is that these Transatlantic innovators belong to a different family, which can only be called that of the poets, if you mean by a poet a performer who does everything except write poetry.

BYPASS: We can leave that argument, if you agree for the moment, till you have heard what I have to say in explanation of what can genuinely be called " Modernist " work. It is sometimes supposed that the group headed by Ezra Pound and F. S. Flint, and including among others H. D. and Richard Aldington, are the forerunners of the new movement. They are, in fact, nothing of the kind. As Mr. Robert Graves says in his book, *A Survey of Modernist Poetry,* " They wanted to express new moods, and in free verse (or cadence). They believed in free verse; and to believe in one way of writing poetry as against another is to have the attitude of a quack rather than of a scientist towards one's art and to be in a position of selling one's ideas rather than of constantly submitting them to new tests. Authentic advanced poetry of the present day differs from such programmes for poetry in this important respect: that it is concerned with a reorganisation of the matter, rather than the manner of poetry." In other words, the failure of the Imagists was the same as that of Swinburne, though, as the group produced nobody comparable to him in poetic receptivity, none of them is likely to share his limited immortality. The Imagists were at war with the accepted forms of poetry, not because they were not suitable to their view of life, but on a general theory that they were universally unsuitable. In a sense it is true that these forms have become universally unsuitable, but that fact cannot be established by theory, but only by experiment. It might happen (though God forbid that it should) that a real poet would arise who would only express himself in the triolet and the ballade. In that improbable event life would adapt itself to that mode. But, of course, it

200

will not happen. Art does not turn back on itself. Like life itself, it is for ever moving on, and, like life itself, for ever adapting, altering, and new.

MYSELF: Like the 50,000,000-year-old ant found in amber which was identical in every particular with the contemporary insects.

BYPASS: I am not discussing evolution, but progress, which is quite a different thing.

MYSELF: Quite, in that it has no shadow of scientific foundation.

BYPASS: All science is a many-coloured guess in the dark. Artistic truth bases itself on statements made in the white radiance of eternity. I repeat, therefore, that the Imagists were Conservatives offering themselves for re-election as Radicals on the ground that, though their principles remained unchanged, they looked different. Indeed, it is interesting to observe that one by one, as they examined their own hearts, they either ceased to write at all, or wrote like Richard Aldington in *Fool i' the Forest*, work which was plainly derived from *Waste-Land* and the true Modernist movement. Aldington, it may be assumed, had come to realise that you could not change a fox-terrier into a bull-dog merely by wagging his tail for him. Indeed, that the only result of such an attempt would probably be a severe bite. He saw that the poet must go back to life itself, and ask of it to dictate the forms of poetry.

Aldington, as a matter of fact, could only see life darkly in T. S. Eliot's looking-glass, but that half-glimpse was worth the whole of the Imagist philanderings with verse which was only free in the sense that a bolting horse is free. Because you cannot impose order or form upon a living organism from without. That can only come from within.

I do not delay with the Georgians, quite properly classified by Robert Graves as a dead movement. They a little resemble the pre-Raphaelites, who went back to the wrong painters before Raphael for their models. The Georgians, who may be described generally as pre-Tennysonians, probably regarded Wordsworth as their spiritual ancestor. He was, but it was the Wordsworth of the *We Are Seven* and *The Daffodils* and not the Wordsworth (who alone matters) of *The Prelude*. They believed (as Wordsworth recovering from his indiscretion in France may have believed) that a milk-pail on a mountain had some intrinsic quality superior to that of a four-wheel cab on London Bridge. Nothing could, of course, be further from the truth. "The country," observed Mr. Raddles in *Pickwick Papers,* "for a wounded spirit." We cannot on this occasion fail to sympathise with Mrs. Raddles's spirited rejoinder, who bade Raddles hold his peace lest she should forget her sect and strike him. There is no refuge from life, no anodyne for mortality. The poet must plunge into life, not seek to escape it. And the Georgians, who were perhaps consciously seeking a refuge from the increasing complexities of contemporary existence in week-end cottage pastoralism, suffered the fate of all refugees. They lost their own country and they could find no domicile in any other. Fortunately, they did not produce any figure sufficiently vital to repeat the reactionary dictatorship of Tennyson. They shuffled the pack of English verse uneasily, but they never dealt it. A more rigorous set of players in the persons of the Sitwell family in England, and in T. S. Eliot, E. E. Cummings, Crow Ransom, and Archibald Macleish in the United States, cut in on the game.

MYSELF: Perhaps, before you continue, you will tell me what the game is, and what the denominations of the cards. Do you still distinguish, for example, between the ace and the deuce and between hearts and spades? Or is there only one card and only one colour?

BYPASS: The cards and the game are the same; we have only changed the names slightly. The romantics called their types kings and queens; we call them men and women. As to the colour, we see no reason why they should not be universally red. And the game is still life, which with us is not a synonym for death.

I do not propose to give a general exposition of the methods of Modernism. I will only say that it traces the poet-thought to its origin, releases it, and then endows it with independent existence. I do not think it necessary to waste time upon the typographical devices which many Modernists have been compelled to adopt in order to drive their meaning home. Much vacuous laughter has been excited, particularly by such expedients as printing letters in the middle of the word as capitals, by detaching the final S from a plural noun and printing it in a line by itself, by omitting punctuation. All that is only an attempt to restore virginity to syntax. Metaphysicians constantly complain that their work is seriously hampered by having to use words ruined and obliterated by the friction of innumerable associations, like coins worn by circulation. They are driven, in consequence, to invent, as scientists are similarly driven to invent, large lumbering words which, in spite of their inherent ugliness, do accurately correspond to their meaning. The poet is in even worse case. Not only have his words been debauched by centuries of daily handling, but they have been rouged and powdered by generations of poets. They stand in hesitating rows like a multitude of anile dowagers pitifully hiding their fallen chaps under paint, and holding out long claw-like hands in a heart-breaking imitation of the cool gestures of youth. The typographical innovations, though not an essential of the Modernist movement, do at least shake up the mind of the reader, and refuse to allow him to take for granted words — those sacred and mysterious visitors, those angels descending upon Lot, for whose heavenly persons the misguided mob incessantly clamours. In the result, when you read a poem such as *Sunset,* by Cummings (the poem to

204

which Graves devotes so much attention), the reader is obliged first to make the acquaintance of each word as though he were meeting it for the first time, yes, and even, on occasion, of each letter. By that one trick (which is solely for the reader's and not at all for the poet's benefit) its primitive astonishments are restored to language. Like M. Jourdain, the common man awakes with a start of ecstasy to realise that all his time, while he believed he was merely talking, he has, in fact, been speaking, and speaking at times something which is not merely prose but actually poetry.

That is one considerable point gained. You will see that so far from being a lock it is a key. But a key to what? A key to a world of thought in which poetry is no longer a craft but an organism, a world where the poet may prune his trees or water his flowers, but where he recognises that the seed of the singer is less than the earth on which it falls. The Modernist has discovered that life is a better poet than he is. His function is to let life have its way.

Let me, in confirmation of this, quote from the preface of *are 5,* by Cummings, in which reluctantly he explains what he is at. " It is with roses and locomotives (not to mention acrobats, Spring, electricity, Long Island, the 4th of July, the eyes of mice, and Niagara Falls) that my ' poems ' are competing. They are also competing with each other, with elephants, and with *Il Greco.*" He means that to make poetry is an act of parenthood, or at least of physical manufacture. The

Modernist is not so foolish as to pretend that the poet does not play a part, even a dominating part, in the production of his poem. But he admits his subject into partnership. He does not force his products by imposing some pre-established and arbitrary form. He does not, in a word, send his poems to a Public School in order that, losing their individuality, they may be moulded into a uniform type. He allows them to grow and develop in accordance with their character and desire.

So much for the general outline. So far as the particular is concerned, just as the Modernist uses a deliberately new typography in order to revive syntax, so in his substance he goes back to the primitive value of words and thoughts themselves, and does not smother them with useless epithets, similes, metaphors, rhyme-cadence, and all the poetic fancy-dress of the poetical poet. His idea of verse is not that of a Venetian masquerade staged in the Albert Hall. He resolves thought into its elements. The result on the reader's mind at first blush is the same as that produced by his typography — a sense of bewilderment; and, in the feebler, of resentment. But here again in a profounder sense the Modernist poet will not permit his public to take his poem for granted. They must make an effort in order to share the almost rude realities detached by the poet. Illumination can only be attained here, as always, by the stripped spirit at the price of prayer and fasting. The mind is not offered the easy way of religion by the greased paths of vestments, incense, stained-glass windows, self-consciously smooth organ, and a plausible priest. Worship must be on bare benches under bare walls. There are no tricks and no inducements. But if the worshipper will persist he will find that here at last he has attained to the Communion of Saints.

MYSELF: I have listened to you, Bypass, not only with interest but with respect. But I confess that in all this there is one thing that escapes me. What distinction do you draw in this new world between poetry and prose? Even if I were prepared to accept your other brilliant fallacies, I should still have to press that question. Because it seems to me that, however convincing your theory may be, it tends in the long run to obliterate the distinction and lead to the conclusion that for the Modernist, as for Boileau, the final commendation of poetry is to pronounce it *beau comme la prose.*

May I in this connection quote the following poem by Miss Marianne Moore?

Openly, yes
with the naturalness
of the hippopotamus or the alligator
when it climbs out on the bank to experience the

Sun, I do these
things which I do, which please
no one but myself. Now I breathe and now I am
sub-

> *merged; the blemishes stand up and shout when*
>   *the object*
>
> *In view was a*
> *renaissance; shall I say*
>   *the contrary? the sediment of the river which*
>   *encrusts my joints, makes me very gray but I am*
>   *used. . . .*

I can, I think, quite clearly follow Miss Moore's meaning. It may be profound, though it seems to me to be infantile. But what I do not understand is why it should be called poetry, nor do I know how, for example, you distinguish between Mr. Cummings at his most breathless, and Miss Stein. Is there any means left of recognising poetry as such?

BYPASS: If an answer were required to that question the Modernist would ask in return how you distinguish between the Song of Solomon and De Quincey at his best. The reply would, I suppose, be that the difference is that between hitting a gong and rubbing it. The poem is the hammer-stroke, prose is the smoother application of the palm.

MYSELF: That, my dear Bypass, is a mere evasion.

BYPASS: It is no more an evasion than Christ's answer to Pilate. Truth is the divine Person, and the only answer is to exhibit it. If you do not believe, you could regard the retort as blasphemy or a confession of failure.

If you do believe, you will see that it is the only rejoinder that could have any meaning.

MYSELF: In other words, then, there is no criterion except individual conviction? Well, that is no doubt true of all artistic apperception.

You say that the Modernist poet does not mould, but releases, life, and you explain the devices he adopts to restore, in your phrase, virginity to syntax. But what do you in fact mean by that? In what does the Modernist poet differ in that regard, say, from Keats when he wrote *The Ode to the Nightingale?* Do you imagine that Keats knew in advance exactly how life was going to shape itself? Do you deny that when he wrote

> *The same that oft times hath*
> *Charmed magic casements opening on the foam*
> *Of perilous seas in fairy lands forlorn*

he was not restoring the virginity of the untroubled moon to syntax? Did he not force his reader to make the most difficult effort of all, to cut clean away from the casual futilities of current life, and face unresolved loveliness?

And if that is true — and I do not see how you can deny it — then I am entitled to say that the aim of Keats was identical with what you tell me is the aim of Mr. Cummings. You will perhaps reply that Keats muffled his beauty with an elaborately decorated veil of scansion and metre. In the same way life muffles the daffodil by imposing on her a pre-arranged gold ballet-skirt, and a green-stocking toe, in the same way Zeus ruined Helen by confining her in the stereotyped mould of a woman.

Surely that isn't true. Surely the mould is subdued to the material that is poured into it. If you seek to educate a child, whatever freedom or independence you seek to give him, you do not wish him to have the freedom of a vacuum, or the independence of a tree. There are certain irreducible minima with which you start. In the case of a child, humanity and human limitations. In the case of a poem the *à priori* distinction between poetry and all other forms of art. Keats was not hampered by that limitation any more than a great teacher is hampered by the fact that his pupil is a child and not a proposition in Euclid.

The result is that what Keats produces is a poem recognisable as such. Your Modernists, if their aim is, as you admit, the same as that of Keats, must stand or fall by the same test. You reply that they do. To which I say that you will find that, just as Edith Sitwell increasingly uses the traditional shapes to exhibit her discoveries, so your Cummings and Marianne Moore will, if they are poets and not impostors, in the long run pour their new wine into the old bottles. Because at the end of all you can only remove the distinction between verse and prose at the risk of destroying one, if not both.

BYPASS: My dear Humbert, assertion is not proof.

MYSELF: No, Bypass. That is why I ask for poetry from the Modernists. But I see that we are both tired and that we should do well to postpone my reply, as they say in Parliamentary circles, to a later occasion.

BYPASS: Very well, let us dine next Wednesday. That will give you the opportunity of meeting my spontaneous exposition with carefully prepared debating rejoinder.

We met as arranged the following Wednesday in Bypass's rooms. We wasted no time upon preliminaries. I'll go back, I said, Bypass, to the point which I had reached, and begin, if I may, by examining your premises.

I understand these to be that the poet must make the poem live for and in itself, and the reader of it think for himself. When reduced to that level it seems to me to be not much more than saying that the real poet has something new to say, and will, in consequence and of necessity, say it in a new way. That is a platitude, but platitudes are, in general, universal truths neglected, and never acted upon. Indeed, it is not a paradox to say that it is the successive business of all original thinkers in every age to restore the eternal authority of the platitude. It is no criticism of the Modernists, therefore, to assert that their whole doctrine is founded on this platitude. On the contrary, it is to recognise that their theory deserves respectful attention.

But it is not enough to have rediscovered a platitude — it is necessary also to study its application. The Modernists, without asserting that rhyme and cadence have become impossible to a true poet, imply that we have reached a point where originality can only with the profoundest difficulty overcome these initial restrictions. Cadence, for example, through which the Imagists believed verse might find salvation, they brush aside as merely a new variety of handcuffs. Let me, therefore, examine your two practical suggestions for the future of verse — that represented by typography, and the other by intellectual ellipsis.

I recognise, of course, that, as you yourself said, the typographical methods of such writers as Cummings and Miss Moore are not more than a device to attract or to startle the reader's attention. You will observe, therefore, that they serve exactly the same purpose as the traditional scheme of printing verse in separate lines. As a mere matter of practice, the reader is jerked into unusual attention by the fact that the prose page is deliberately cut up and re-assorted. The first printer therefore who set up verse in the form that we know it had anticipated Mr. Cummings. But you will reply that after all these centuries that particular device has long since lost its quality of surprise. Indeed, the wheel has come full circle, and poetry is now only surprising if not presented in the traditional form. That may be true (though I shall hope to show in a moment that the traditional form contains something intrinsically valuable), but an obvious criticism occurs to me: one of two things must happen to the typography — either it will in turn become traditional, or be abandoned as inconvenient. It can have no intrinsic value in itself. On the contrary, the belief that it has such a value reveals a formidable fallacy. It suggests that the isolated word or letter, apart from the poet's use of it, has some value. That is materialism run mad. It is an attempt to restore that independence to the object, the domination of which is precisely the object of art.

BYPASS: One moment. Are you taking refuge in the old Idealist obscurantism? A poet can no more dominate words than a painter colour. He can at best conspire with them, so as to give them their own life. The essence of Modernism is to recognise that verse is not a tyranny, but a partnership between the artist and his material.

MYSELF: Or to phrase it differently, the poet, finding that he cannot manage his medium, submits in part to its direction, as though an architect should fail to introduce a staircase into the house because the timber was unwilling. No, believe me, there is here a fundamental point. Words are not destroyed by the poet, nor can they be created. And no word can hope to enter the kingdom of verse unless it is born again in the spirit of the poet. If you maintain that the word has an independent right, you are oddly enough going beyond the wildest conceptions of the traditional poet. He is often accused of accommodating his work to the necessities of metre and rhyme. He would be the first to admit that, so far as he does this, he is a bad poet. But the Modernist apparently insists on an absolute slavery to the whim of a single consonant. That suggests a morbid passion for self-humiliation only previously exhibited by the Flagellants.

BYPASS: You are deliberately confusing the issue. The Modernist regards himself as absolutely free to adjust the word to his need. He can disregard rhythm, rhyme, punctuation —

MYSELF: and grammar —

BYPASS: and what is called grammar, if necessary. His sole object is to state exactly and finally what he has in mind. But he is not so foolish as to suppose that the word in itself does not exist. On the contrary, one of his great discoveries is that it does exist. He places it, but he does not disembowel it. He presses its unresolved qualities into his service, so that for the first time the secret essence of the word is mixed in the poet's chaldron.

MYSELF: It is a pathetic picture that you paint — not of slavery but of enfranchisement. You are composing a new *Uncle Tom's Cabin,* in which the words trodden into the swamps by Shakespeare, mutilated by Milton, and flogged by Shelley and Keats, are given their man-

214

hood by Mr. Cummings, the last of the liberators. You see the unhappy wretches in disordered masses huddling in the steerage of ocean-going vessels. Having eluded the attention of Ellis Island, they kiss the sacred soil, enriched by Mr. Cummings, and at last, standing upright, cry "Freedom!" And they reward Mr. Cummings, as they used to reward Humpty Dumpty, by doing exactly what he tells them. But it seems to me that Mr. Cummings, and those who fail to think with him, are, as I suggested above, exposing themselves to all the difficulties of indiscriminate enfranchisement. They begin to find that words that, in the good old slave-days of Shakespeare, did what they were told even gladly, now have views of their own. They insist, for example, on being treated, it seems, like "acrobats, Spring, electricity, Long Island, the 4th of July, the eyes of mice, and Niagara Falls." These are obviously serious, if perhaps slightly incongruous, claims. But you will observe the very real embarrassment in which Mr. Cummings finds himself. He desires, for example, to write a poem on "Sunset." He appeals to the words that have some relation to that phenomenon. But they indignantly repudiate him. They are busy elsewhere, either on a trapeze, gilding the lily, regulating dynamos, enjoying cocoa-nut shies, celebrating American independence, watching the cat, or being tumultuously drowned. They invite Mr. Cummings to look elsewhere, to find unemployed words, which have never been used for this purpose, or, if possible, for any purpose whatever before. Mr. Cummings has, it is true, escaped the tyrannies of rhyme, metre, and even sense. But here is a new and almost unbearable domination. "Well," he says, "what words may I have?" and he is presented with the following:

"Stinging gold swarms upon the spire; silver chant the litanies; the great bells are ringing with rose, the lewd, fat bells; and a tall wind is dragging the sea with dreams." "They don't mean much," says Mr. Cummings despondently. "That's your affair," say the words; and "O my God," they add, "here's the cat!" But Mr. Cummings is not of the stuff to be baffled by a mouser. "Very well," he says, "I'll use these words if they're all that I am allowed, and the reader shall do the rest." This raises the further question whether the new poetry should not be anonymous, leaving to every reader who understands it the right to append his name at least as part-author. In this case one reader apparently understands the poem to indicate

    (1) that the salt air stings the poet's face;
    (2) that the sun is touching the sea with gold like swarms of bees;
    (3) that it is lifting tall spires,
    (4) so that the sound of bells is audible chanting litanies to rosy windows; and
    (5) a wind is dragging the sea like a net.

If that is a just interpretation (and I have no doubt that it may be) then it would seem that the words have treated Mr. Cummings very shabbily. It seems grossly unfair of "lewd" to have forced its way in. Why shouldn't it have been content with Long Island, and why should "fat" have imposed itself on the poet? They might urge that they serve the same purpose as a misleading clue in an acrostic. But Mr. Cummings is entitled to say that the thing was quite difficult enough without this added complexity. But in any case you will agree that without the reader the poem is almost helpless. It is not unfair, therefore, that the completed effort should bear the joint signature of the setter and the solver of the puzzle.

Bypass: All this is, no doubt, very clever. But you have neither examined the theory honestly, nor have you explained why all contemporary verse, except the Modernist, is dead. We are not claiming that we write great poetry, because we do not assert that the great figure has yet appeared. But we do claim that we write living poetry. And one proof is that you, like all other traditionalists, are provoked to use the last weapon of the defeated reactionary confronted by a new idea — vulgar ridicule. If we are to continue this discussion at all, I must ask you to treat your opinion seriously or —

Myself: Like Delarue, you will plunge into the pines. Very well, let us be serious. There is no theory behind this movement in the sense of a genuine metaphysical basis. You may reply that that is true of all verse. I admit it, but the point of difference is that here the poets are claiming such a basis. But assume that it has been thought out, what does it imply or contend? It revives, without understanding them, all the old Realist fallacies. It dismisses, without presumably having heard of it, the whole Idealist contention. This is obviously not the time or place to enter into metaphysical argument. Nor am I prepared (even if I were capable) of disposing of the Mathematic-realist, the creative evolutionary, and the pseudo-philosophical psycho-analytical schools of thought. I merely observe that to evolve a true theory of æsthetic is no less difficult, and has almost as long a controversial history as the evolution of a theory of cognition. There is no finality in either, and it would be equally arrogant and foolish to proclaim any single theory — for example the Idealist — as necessarily right. But at least if metaphysics are to be prayed in aid, they must be true metaphysics. It is not sufficient to read a popular hand-book on relativity, or even to have read Freud in the original. Metaphysics is not the result of bright inspirations after dinner in Soho. It is of all human endeavour that demanding the most resolute, the most unremitting, and the most patient of thought. You cannot begin a metaphysical theory on the assumption that Plato, Descartes, Liebnitz, Spinoza, Berkeley, Hume, Kant, and Hegel never existed. You might as well dispense with the whole heritage of life, and announce that you would live as though you were the first man. It follows therefore that nursery metaphysics and schoolroom theories of æsthetic will have no value, except as illuminating the personality of their

218

authors. They may be witty, they may be well-written, they may be the result of profound conviction. But that will not make then philosophy. You cannot think by adding cubits to your stature, like the frog in the fable. You will only end by bursting — probably into an explosion of temper.

I do not therefore attempt (even if I could) a metaphysical reply. For you cannot argue with an undistributed middle or with Wednesday week. You can only answer assertion by reducing it to its logical absurdity, and that I suggest. I have at least attempted in the examination of the claim put forward on behalf of Mr. Cummings. But there is another danger of quite a different kind in this doctrinaire approach to the craft of verse. If it were only bad metaphysics, it might be dismissed, but when it is applied metaphysics it becomes a more serious matter. It is always dangerous when artists attempt to create to a theory. I am not, of course, pretending that the poet, like every other creator, can avoid a serious examination of the theory of his art, or of the practice of his predecessors. He will learn a great deal from that study, and indeed without it he may be regarded as uneducated. But it is quite a different thing deliberately to set out to prove a poetic theory in practice. If a poet really can write traditional poetry, then nothing is more hazardous than to refuse to do so, because some inchoate semi-philosophic theory throws a doubt on the basis of the tradition. The poet must learn his trade, but, having learned it, he must

write as he is and feels, and not as he thinks he ought
to be. If he falls into that error he will be deliberately
stultifying his own genius. Let him by all means invent
a new form, but only if that form is the inevitable expression of his own personality, and not because he is
intellectually convinced that the old forms are wrong.

BYPASS: How do you know that that is not the secret
of the Modernist forms?

MYSELF: By the results, which show either that the
writers are not poets or are poets trapped in a morass.
I return to what I said about the management of words.
The master of his art dictates to his words. He listens
to no nonsense from them. He puts them where they
are needed; and they gladly respond to some inevitable
rightness in his disposition. But the bad poet of all kinds
is at the mercy of his words and his medium. He is
stampeded by them into inversions, strained phrases,
clumsy movements, and every sort of evasion of the
ultimate simplicity of complete control. The words
pursue and hunt him into corners, from which he
emerges by surrendering to their improper demands.
He is for ever paying the Danegeld of obscurity or
poeticism. The Modernist poet — or those with whom
I am acquainted — seems of all poets the most helpless
before the turbulent conspiracy of the unbroken droves
of words. He sees words like " rose," " nightingale,"
" beauty," " Helen," " Troy," and a thousand others
sweeping up and down with a great train of glittering

association. He assumes in advance that he cannot sub-
due them to his purpose. He feels that he will be carried
away by them like a mediæval knight caught in the
heavy trappings of his horse in the lists. He decides
therefore to banish them, and to look for words that,
like a good woman, have no history. But that is to
confess defeat from the outset. There is no word so
worn but that it can be re-invested with life, if genius
breathes it, no form so hackneyed but that inspiration
can re-establish it. It is, of course, not easy: indeed it
is impossible for everybody except for the master. He
will not fear, but rather rejoice in the difficulties of
tradition. He will make the rose smell as sweet by the
same name, and the nightingale recharm casements as
magic over seas no less forlorn. I do not say that he
must use the old forms. I gladly concede that T. S.
Eliot in " The Hollow Men " has abundantly justified
a new form. But I do say that the new form is not in
itself necessarily the way of salvation, nor the old necessarily the path to Gehenna.

Bypass: At least attempt some proof. On my side I
have all that is admitted to be new and vigorous in
poetry — Herbert Read, Edith Sitwell, T. S. Eliot, Conrad Aiken, and Archibald Macleish. They have proved
that the new form alone is appropriate to modern life.
Where are the apostles of the old?

Myself: They have proved nothing of the kind. They
have proved only that they have a slightly different way

of achieving the old result, but where they succeed they succeed in the oldest way of all — the imposition upon chaos of some wisp of order. They do not flounder after their words in slavish obedience. When they achieve anything permanent they are as dictatorial and as uncompromisingly poetical as Keats. And before I examine the latest book which W. B. Yeats — after all, a contemporary poet — has written, let me put one more point of view: I have never been able to understand why in the year 1920 a violent break in the whole continuity of verse became inevitable. I could see no similar earthquake in any other art, or in any other period. You said earlier that this movement had been steadily developing in all the arts since the 'nineties. But don't you actually mean just the opposite of that? Every art has progressed vitally since the 'nineties — the novel, painting, architecture, and verse. But in every case, however violent the change might appear to be superficially, in fact it has been an even faithful development of tradition. There is nothing in E. M. Forster which would have offended Jane Austen, Monet and Manet could be hung by the side of Constable without conflict, the town-hall at Stockholm could have been built next door to the Pitti Palace without incongruity. But could you print

> *. . . some*
> *guys talk big*
> *about Lundun Burlin an gay Paree an*

222

some guys claims der never was
nutn like Nooer Leans Shikagho Sain
Looey Noo York an' San Fran dictaphones
wireless subways vacuum
cleaners pianolas funnygraphs skyscrapers and safety
*   razors*
Sall right in its way kiddo
but as for I gimme de good old daze

by the side of

Tears, idle tears, I know not what they mean,

and in particular as a parallel to

O life in death the days that are no more.

I am not for the moment asking which is the better.
I am simply observing that the two pieces of work
have no more relation than the Arc de Triomphe and
" Yes, we have no bananas." It is not development: it
is a transfer to a new dimension. It may be right that
there should be such a transfer. But, if it is, one of two
things follows — either the best of Tennyson should
not be called poetry, or, alternatively, that gold name
should not be applied to the work of Mr. Cummings.
You will, of course, apply the usual blackmail, and tell
me that, like all other reactionaries, I cannot or will
not recognise the advent of what is to supersede me.
In reply to that I advance the Greek Anthology, which
covers 1,200 years of verse. There is no good verse

223

written in A.D. 600 which Sappho would not have understood, and nothing first-rate in 600 B.C. which was not acceptable after the barbarians had swept over Rome and the West. You may say that that proves that poetry stood still for twelve centuries. I answer that, if that is so, the heart of man stood still by its side, and is still standing there.

BYPASS: All the more reason for waking the Sleeping Beauty.

MYSELF: O generation of fairy princes, what is your answer to de la Mare and W. B. Yeats? If the old words and the old forms are outworn, how do you explain away *The Old Angler* and *The Last Coachload*? If we must abandon beauty as Meleager and Simonides understood it, what is the reply to *Sailing to Byzantium*, published in the year 1928 by Yeats, from which I quote the last verse:

> *Once out of nature I shall never take*
> *My bodily form from any natural thing,*
> *But such a form as Grecian goldsmiths make*
> *Of hammered gold and gold enamelling*
> *To keep a drowsy emperor awake;*
> *Or set upon a golden bough to sing*
> *To lords and ladies of Byzantium*
> *Of what is past, or passing, or to come.*

Is that not the same voice that sang the choruses of Sophocles, or cried loudly in the deeps of Inferno? It

224

is plain and it is simple. It has the rhythms as certain as the movement of water in wind. It has the music of those waters heard at night. Why must it be exchanged for the noise of a can rattled on cobbles? Because if Cummings is right, then Yeats is wrong. And if Yeats is wrong, then, like the Goths at Constantinople, we had better burn the libraries of the world. We had better stand on the dark walls of that last outpost of civilisation, and, watching the red death of all recorded loveliness, look out into the night, and see as the flames fall the first great shadow of the Dark Ages.

BYPASS: And so in the end you fling a handful of confetti in the face of the public and think that you will blind them. But I tell you that the time has come when the world has a right to think and feel for itself. The time has come when it will not take its emotions pre-digested, and emasculated. The reader will think for himself, and feel for himself, and he will spurn the prepared beauties of traditional elegances for the painted prostitutes that they are. The Modernist poet will make an honest woman of Euterpe.

MYSELF: And in ten years' time a new poet will arise and cry:

> *What ailed us, oh gods, to desert you*
> *For creeds that refuse and restrain.*
> *Come down and redeem us from virtue,*
> *Our Lady of Pain.*

You cannot bind Euterpe to any wedlock. She is not for any single man, because, though she is the same for ever, for every true lover she is new and fresh and incredible. And the truth is, Bypass, that if among you Modernists there is a true poet, when his last word is written, and he looks into her eyes, he will see, dark and irrevocable, the tumbling walls of Troy.

BYPASS: Then he will have failed.

MYSELF: All poets fail. That is why there is always room for another.

"DRUM"

"Drum"

I WAS THINKING of an evening with my English master — Barton — and with Albert Rutherston in a first-floor room in (I think it was called) Lindum Terrace at Bradford. It was a dull February evening, and the room, except for the presence of books and of my two mentors, was like that in any other moderately well-kept lodging-house. The wall-paper in particular, as I remember, had that curious quality of apparently premeditated delirium, typical of industrial thought. There was whisky for the grown-ups on the little side-table, which suffered from rickets, and on the side-board that shouldered its way half-way across the room, like a Cubist conception of a rhinoceros, was a glass lemon-squeezer for me. It was raining on the roofs, it was raining on the town. But in my heart was a sun as tall as Everest. I was seventeen and this was an evening with the gods.

Barton was not merely an Oxford man in Bradford. He was not, that is to say, merely vowed to, and a part of, all the things that the warehouses sullenly repudiated. He had not merely won the Newdigate Verse Prize for a poem in heroic couplets on *Gibraltar*. He did not merely pronounce his " a's " and " o's " long in a world where, in order to save time and therefore money, they were savagely abbreviated. But he was actually a writer of articles in *The Saturday Review,* that emblem of the great world of letters. There was positively lying by the side of the tantalus, an envelope which I couldn't help seeing, which bore on the flap the sacred name. He was, it appeared, in correspondence with that journal on as easy a footing as I might be with the Secretary of the Leeds Grammar School Football Club. Small wonder if I hugged myself.

And Albert? Well, Albert was a different affair. I couldn't remember the time when I hadn't known him. In spite of his advantage in years, we had, it seemed, always played together, and I had a hundred pictures of him in my mind, all the more striking by contrast with this emancipated and laurelled creature, who had returned to Bradford no less a figure than a Slade scholar. I saw him, for example, proudly lying in his bed after having hewed his leg in half with an axe, when he had gone out " chumping " for wood against the 5th of November. He had, I remembered, been given an exceptionally green fort to console him. But he did not require consolation. He was able to assure me, on the contrary, that Dr. Bronner had taken the view that another inch, and he would have lost his leg. Or I observed him with awe strolling down Mount Royde on his way to the same doctor, negligently informing the world that he had a fishbone about a foot long stuck in his throat. Or later I had a vision of him in the large bare Art room bending over a sheet of paper about the same size as himself, industriously drawing with his left hand. He had somehow escaped from the lessons, which he could never learn, to the one in which he could teach even Mr. Bergan — the Art Master — a great deal. And that at fifteen.

And now that small and radiant creature, more like a brightly varnished toy than a human boy, had returned at twenty-one a demigod. His profession was painting. He lived in a studio, surrounded by London and painters. He knew Max Beerbohm, and (he let it be known casually) had supped (astounding metropolitan phrase!) with a Frenchman by the name of Rodin. And a week before he had read to me with a certain minuscular majesty, a work by a poet of his acquaintance — *Dolores*. I do not know whether I was more excited by *Our Lady of Pain,* or by the fact that Albert knew its author. A poet — not dead like all poets of whom I had previously heard, and what a poet, Tennyson, Keats, Shelley and Shakespeare rolled into one. And Albert knew him. I goggled.

Well! I was thinking of that decisive evening in Lindum Terrace. Barton and Albert were, with immense distinction, drinking whisky, and in between the sips talking to each other and occasionally to me in the large accent of the early gods. "Of what was it spoken, of what was it told?" Art, and literature, as between two professors of those magics. There was, it seemed, an astonishing revival in both. Albert spoke of an association called the New English Art Club, which had replaced an older organisation disgracefully known as the Royal Academy. (Barton, I think, laughed with gentle amusement at the mention of that infamous Society. I laughed also, but furtively, lest I might be doing the wrong thing. But I needn't have worried. They weren't thinking of me.) He recited a series of names, most of them like the monosyllabic cracks of a whip — John, Max, Steer, Tonks, my brother Will — and Uncle Tom Rembrandt and all. Albert, though enthusiastic, was judicial. It was not open to question that they were the greatest of all English painters. The question argued with impartiality was whether they were better than the French Impressionists, and therefore the best of all time. My view, never having seen their work, or that of their rivals, or indeed any paintings at all, except Will's and Albert's, was for what it was worth that they certainly were. I was indeed prepared to say so, but I decided to limit myself to a sympathetic expression. Barton, observing it, told me to get myself a lemon-squash. He may have misunderstood it. I hadn't at that time had much practice in looking sympathetic.

Barton, on his side, was equally convinced that the great age of letters had returned. There was a man, Bennett — Albert knew him of course? — of whom more would be heard, and Wells — my God, what a marvel! (I gasped, bearing in mind that he wrote in

232

the popular magazines. Was it possible that literature could appear there! Grave doubts as to all my standards began to creep over me.) And then the late dramatic critic of *The Saturday* — an Irishman, Bernard Shaw. He, it appeared, was content to range himself by the side of Shakespeare. This was perhaps an unduly modest estimate. I had almost interjected Kipling, when I was anticipated by a wholesale denunciation of that impostor — the author of " The Absent-Minded Beggar." I reddened in my corner at the narrowness of my escape. But it was all right. Max, it seemed, was going to deal with Kipling. And poetry! Swinburne, of course, but he belonged to another Age. There were the new men. Barton took down a book by one Walter Ramal, a young thing in the twenties, and Albert knew the author of *Marpessa*. This was almost too much for me. Last week Swinburne: to-night Ramal, and Stephen Phillips. I was almost sick.

Barton perhaps observed that I was in an unusual condition. I had written a poem in the school magazine — the Bradfordian — on the passing of the Steam-Tram from the streets of the town. It was a lament in the manner of Lycidas containing among other memorable lines these:

Now, now no longer shall the aged sire
Rush forth to greet thee, and embrace the mire.
No more shall matron, peering through the damp,
Threat thy conductor with infuriate gamp.

233

It was certain, Barton suggested, that I had written others. I almost stammered in my anxiety to demonstrate that I also belonged to the period. I had committed my poems, like a misdemeanour in secret, and now I was becoming a part of a Renascence. Perhaps, they would like to hear, but they wouldn't like to hear. They wanted to tell me, not to listen. They were grave, but full of fire. This was an astonishing age for the painter and the poet, if they would grasp their opportunities. Victorianism and decadence were dead and damned. It was an age of active and violent creation. Muirhead Bone was drawing scaffolding, Sickert was busy in the couloirs of " The Middlesex " Musical Hall, Will had rediscovered the ancient civilisation of the Jews, and John had taken the world to pieces and was putting it together again with gigantic leisurely ease, audibly purring. Not less in literature, said Barton, Wells was living so hard that he had burst the present into five hundred years on, Bennett — greater than Æneas — was founding Five Towns all at once, while on the other hand the unspeakable Barrie was fiddling about the Kailyard while the new world burned into life and beauty. *Allons, camarade!* they cried, but heavens! I needed little enough encouragement.

We were standing at the front-door now after that immense exaltation, Barton, slim and tall, his nose still quivering at the tip as it did in moments of excitement, Albert, like a small plump exclamation mark made by a camel-hair brush, and I — well, I can reconstruct

234

myself from photographs, disagreeably fat, my hair parted in the middle, my clothes for some reason always too short in the arms. But what the photographs don't show is my mouth wide open, and my eyes wider still, simply gulping down the dark street, the flickering gas-lamps, and the indifferent rain. " Affirmation — that's the word — affirmation," said Barton, and then went in slamming the door behind him.

" Affirmation? " I crossed Manningham Lane at a gallop, swarmed down Parkfield Road, and climbed up the two flights to my attic bedroom at Oak Mount. From its window I looked clean across the railway-line to the sprawling bulk of a hill — a dumpy spur. I used to think of the range that culminates in the 2,000 feet of Beamsley Beacon. The hill was dark at night except for the one light that I knew was the window of the dour scraggy farmhouse near the top. I put out the gas, and, snatching paper, began to write. " Affirmation! " Well I would affirm with the best of them. I think in fact I wrote a poem which contained the lines:

> *confederate in a plot*
> *To carry standards through the night,*
> *Bring faith where faith was not.*

I was enrolled.

I was reading the *Evening News* in the smoke-room of the Royal Automobile Club when I thought of that episode. In the next chair to mine an elderly man was drowsing over a book by Edgar Wallace. Beyond him, two others were eagerly discussing some matter in rapt, low voices. From time to time a few words escaped cautiously in my direction, almost as though taking shelter. But I could do little for them, because, though I am not, I hope, a snob, they did not belong to my set of words. They lost themselves disconsolately in the spring sunshine beating in as far as the Junior Constitutional Club over the way would let it. The Junior Constitutionalists intercepted a little of the spring air as well.

The *Evening News* was a normal number. I mean that there were interviews with the mother of a murdered girl, with a man who could play the fiddle with his left foot, and with an expert on peace, whose doctrine, in Mr. E. V. Lucas's famous phrase, appeared to be " To secure a state of permanent peace you must prepare for it by ensuring a state of permanent war." There was a leader violently urging economy on the Government, the Civil Service and the masses. Side by side were the gossip-notes enthusiastically recording a ball at which there had been 10,000 tulips painted blue, and where each of the guests had received some item of jewellery in recognition of the strain involved by their attendance. It is, however, fair to add that with one or two exceptions these guests included none of the classes referred to in the leader. There was no mention of literature or the arts, except that there was a description of a new £2,000,000 building. The name

236

of the architect had, however, escaped the enthusiast for arithmetic who was responsible for it. There was also an advertisement of some new appliance for maintaining a permanent wave in shingled hair. The advertisement took the form of a resolution passed at a Board Meeting and was signed in full by the seven members of the Board. It appeared that these gentlemen felt it incumbent on them to testify publicly to their disinterested belief that, as they playfully said, " Britannia rules the waves." They engaged their commercial reputations with that simplicity which must inspire confidence in those who have none. It took the place of such declarations as that of Independence or of the Court of the Jeu de Paume.

I read all this in the spring sunlight without any emotion either of surprise or indignation. I was, after all, middle-aged, and this was the world, full of good fellows (who, it is true, did nothing but harm, but was that their fault?), packed with Rotarians, revolving in vicious circles, gaping at wealth, distressed by the failure of an English boxer to punch an American suddenly in the stomach, aware of the League of Nations as a news item of less importance than greyhound-racing, and eagerly supporting such rival policies of the same journal as " Hats off to France," " Trousers off to Hungary," " Boots off to King Feisul," indeed prepared ultimately to strip altogether, if this would contribute to universal pacification, or war, as the case might be. This was my world, and, if I did not accept it, why was I in exactly that place and in those circumstances reading that particular journal? I was, I think, on the point of sinking into a heavy sleep, when I remembered that evening more than a quarter of a century ago. "Affirmation!" God in Heaven, what had happened to me, and to it?

How did disillusionment begin, and where, and why? Oxford? Surely not Oxford, symbol of all that Bradford denied and resented. Surely not Oxford and New College Lane, where I had wandered the night on which I came up for my scholarship. The cloistral bells rang, boys walked arm in arm with their heads tossed back, and the walls hoarded their beauty even against the conspiracy of the moon. I did not know by what colleges I walked, what towers addressed the air, whither the streets led. I did not need to know. This was farewell to discord, and refusal. To-morrow would be "yes." "Yes," I said, like the girl in "Ulysses": How thick that wall must be — "yes"; look at their white woollen gloves — "yes"; 101 times that big bell called "yes"; just look at that horse-tram — "yes"; and that old man in cap and gown, he must be a don — "yes"; and a man with a harp and a boy singing, "*Still wie die Nacht und tief wie das Meer soll deine Liebe, deine Liebe, sein*" — yes, still as the night and deep as the sea, the love of love — "yes — yes — yes."

But was it "yes"? I remembered Drewitt, the Canning Club, Flecker — John as he was before he changed his name, for some inscrutable reason, to James. Drewitt was my Greats tutor, and I have not since met, and I doubt whether I shall ever again meet, so profound, so vivid, and so cold a mind. He used to sit, hunched in his chair, in the deliberately cheerless second-floor room he had chosen in the disreputable back quad of Wadham — except for that blot, loveliest of colleges. He might (as in fact he later did) have had a room in the front quad, overlooking the great cedar, the three tall limes, and that incorrigible copper-beech in the Fellows' Garden. He might habitually have moistened his arduous days with the very admirable wines that he offered to wholly unappreciative undergraduate guests. But, above all, he might have given the world what he gave a very few, a glimpse into a new order, a guess as startling as Einstein's and reached by processes little less incredible. He might, I mean, have said " yes," but in his ultimate asceticism he denied himself even that indulgence.

I remember the afternoon when he at last made me understand what metaphysics was in fact " about." I cannot impart the secret, because it represents, as it were, a sudden reorganisation of the mind. It is like reversing the spectroscope, and regathering the broken colours into the single white ray. I had been reading Descartes — and, at Drewitt's request, I was fumblingly trying to explain his doctrine. " No," he said suddenly. " No, not: ' I think, therefore I am,' but ' You are not thinking, and therefore you are not.' " I thought desperately of poetry, of emotion, of affirmation. Weren't these also "being"? Were they only spells and incantations? Was truth, was life, the solution of a problem in Euclid? I thought of the fifth proposition — the *Pons Asinorum*. Had I been too much of a donkey to cross it? Apparently, and so farewell to Swinburne, and hail to those dry ghosts, Hume, Kant, and Bradley. I went to my room across the landing (I lived opposite Drewitt), and looked out at the back quad. Gilliat and Marrs shouted up to ask whether I had anything for tea. I had nothing at all, I said. "Well, get something from the J. C. R.," they urged. I went and bought four toasted teacakes and a Windsor cake, and when I came back the kettle had boiled and the tea was ready. "We saw you sneak out of Drewitt's," they observed cheerfully. "Patting his blue-eyed boy on the back, as usual? Too puffed up to consort with Exhibitioners of the B+ grade?" "No," I said, "I don't know that I enjoyed myself. No." "No — Well don't drop the hotters," said Gilliat, "even if you have dropped a brick." "No," I said, and noticed how often the negation had come to my lips.

I blinked my eyes in the Club arm-chair. I'd been asleep, I suppose, but I could almost swear that I saw Drewitt, peering through his thick glasses, behind which his eyes looked black and enormous in his small dead-white face. I don't believe anybody else ever had eyes so bright and so uncommunicative, unless it was Medusa. Shams certainly relapsed into stone under their meditative enquiry. " Shams and what else? " I asked aloud. The elderly gentleman in the next armchair woke with a start, and dropped his Edgar Wallace. He looked at me with well-deserved suspicion. This would never do. I decided to go and dine quietly, but, unhappily, I saw Morrison in the distance, rolling himself slowly up the stairs to the chess-room. " Morrison," I groaned to myself, and so gave up the struggle against reminiscences. After all, Morrison and I had talked, thought, and lived Drewitt for two years together, not least at evening on the terrace of the restaurant above the Neckar or in the long avenues of the Odenwald. Hadn't Morrison dismissed Goethe with a caution, even at his own platform, that looked over pine-woods below the red *Schloss* to the tumbling little town of Heidelberg, that huddled away from the terrors of the forest by its river? " Look," he had said, with a noble gesture, pointing to the hill across the river, and to the path that ascended it, " there climbs the Philosophenweg." No, there was no escape. " I suppose that I had better continue this self-examination," I thought, " though Heaven knows why." But I shall stop on the day when the hansom deposited me at Oxford Station. As the green flag drops, the curtain will drop with it. Unless " Drum " was in the cab with me. But I don't think that he was. Large, gentle, and beloved, he had left Oxford before me. Yes. Oxford ended then, or did it end a month ago when I found the name of Alan Davidson Keith in the obituaries of

The Times? Perhaps. Because for everybody the secret of Oxford is different. For me it was " Drum." I cannot share it with anyone now.

I started on this path by accident. I was trying to find an explanation of the revolt against life, which seems to me to be the dominant note of the day. Having started in an arm-chair, I had better transfer to a desk, and attempt to induce some order upon my reflections. How did metaphysics lead to the Canning Club, where churchwarden pipes were smoked by those with strong stomachs, and where the toast of " Church and State " was drunk over a smoking loving-cup. That, I think, was Drewitt too. To the pure metaphysician all things (as distinct from thoughts) are impure. As an object of cognition there is no ponderable difference between a slum and a palace, or between a stockbroker and a poet. That is not cynicism. It is merely a legitimate attempt to approach, if not truth, then validity, as directly as possible. Reform or alteration is the affair of those who have time for, or interest in, action. The philosopher has no such time nor interest.

Obviously, therefore, the party for a metaphysician was the Conservative, who, like him, substituted re-action for action. Why change anything in the world of appearance, when nothing could happen except in the mind? Moreover, there was Mr. Lloyd George, who came to the Union Society and converted that Assembly, much to its own surprise (and subsequent disgust), to Liberalism. Mr. Lloyd George interfered with cognition. He had apparently read nothing, had the most insensitive approach to life, he practically sobbed when he mentioned mothers or hills, his voice was like buttered toast, his vocabulary was that of the commercial traveller, and yet he had 300 young men all eating the leek before they had even guessed the presence of that Welsh vegetable. I would not eat it — no, not for Cadwallader and all his goats, and, like Pistol, I cried, " I eat and eat, and while I eat, I swear." I didn't recover from the taste for years. I don't know that I have recovered now. I was honoured with an invitation to join the Canning. I joined.

I don't suppose that, with the exception of Mr. Chesterton, any poet has ever been a Conservative, and Mr. Chesterton is a Conservative for every sort of reason that would appeal principally to anarchists. Obviously, creation cannot live with ignoble acceptance. But denial can and does. I should not be surprised if Mr. Cummings in America were a good Republican, or that the Dadaists in France were *camelots du roi.* When everything is going to the dogs, you may as well accompany the movement, and, if possible, lead it. The poet of negation, like the metaphysician, does not challenge life. He merely rejects it. If life responds in kind, that is clearly not the poet's fault.

The curious thing, however, about the Canning was that it contained at least two poets, Julian Grenfell and Patrick Shaw-Stewart. I never knew either of them; but then I never knew anybody in the Canning.

Wolmer, Tavistock, Maidstone — it sounds like a journey on the Southern Railway. I must have attended meetings, because I vaguely remember Lord Hugh Cecil waving about a room in Magdalen like a black flag. There is a photograph, too, of the Club. Grenfell has the queer da Vinci smile at the corner of his mouth that the gods reserve for the fated young. I learned from that association, I think, what Drewitt had already inculcated. A gentleman will not reproach God for not existing. He will be the first to recognise that it is not His fault. I see now that gentlemen, like poets, are born and not made. At the time, I pursued the task of self-manufacture. Nobody in the Canning, I think, believed that I was particularly successful.

And so John (or James) Flecker and Trinity College. Flecker lived in the Trinity cottages that abut on the Broad, and later in a little house hidden away behind St. Saviour's Road. Trinity in his time was in the last degree hearty. They played games with immense success, were simple, and young and strong, and adored the Bishop of London. From time to time agnostics in Balliol poured hot tea on their serious heads, but Trinity retorted by bumping their boat on the river. They bore Balliol no malice, as between good fellows and ex-Public School boys. But the tea-pourers were not in the boat, and — *horrendum dictu* — may not have known that it was bumped. But even the most malicious Trinity man would never have suggested that.

It was in this college that Flecker let it be known that he wrote poetry. Naturally, they tried to hush it (and him) up. Things of that kind might perhaps happen at Pembroke or Wadham or anywhere at Cambridge (and, indeed, if Trinity had known or cared, they were happening rather vigorously in the sister University). They did not happen in a man's college. Flecker, however, was impenitent. His startlingly grey eyes burned in his swarthy face under his straight black hair. He did not conceal his shame or his appearance. He talked rapidly and continuously everywhere to anybody, and he even founded a Club that went by the name of *Les fleurs du mal*. Some members of the Junior Common Room were able to translate that title, and augured the worst. It was supposed that a member of the Senior Common Room realised that it had some reference to a French poet — Baudelaire. But this was a malicious rumour, started either in Wadham or by Beasley at the House. Beasley was capable of starting anything, a revolution, a sonnet, or a New Age. He never cared — brilliant phantom — to do more than start it.

Trinity, like Mr. Kipling's heroes in *Stalky & Co.*, and like them approved by the padre, took action, not overt, or violent, but Action. Flecker unfortunately was thinking of a rhyme for " pallid." The action escaped his notice. I didn't meet him, I think, till my third year, and never became intimate with him. I imagine that he disturbed the Chinese calm appropriate to metaphysical thinking. Undoubtedly he was disturbing. Beasley and he had produced an Eights' week paper called *The Red Man*. They had been reluctantly compelled to omit some of their more concrete flights, but of serious work I seem to remember (though I'm probably wrong) *The Oxford Canal,* and of work in another manner a poem which threw a new light on that little-known monarch Cambyses:

> *King Cambyses*
> *Took several prizes.*
> *One for virility,*
> *And two for amiability.*

In addition Flecker asserted that he was writing a novel, a volume of short stories, and a play. He was also importing white Curaçao, which he had acquired during his visits to Montmartre. " I amuse my French friends," he said, " by imitating the French accent of the English." A philosopher had some difficulty in reassuring himself. But anyhow Flecker was probably inventing the novel and the rest. And if he wasn't, nobody would read them.

Flecker, of course, was no metaphysician. He professed himself, indeed, a Realist. That was only because he thought that it might astonish somebody, or perhaps because Beasley had once said that anything was better than Idealism, or he may have liked Professor Cook-Wilson's white beard, the principal contribution, as I seem to remember, of that distinguished thinker to the theory of cognition. To discuss metaphysics with him was like a paper-chase, with Flecker laying trails in all directions and then forgetting about the race and climbing a tree. No doubt he saw things from that eminence, but they had no connection with episto-mology.

" Drum " was sitting bolt upright in his deep wicker-chair, spraying himself with his patent asthma-curer. His head — of a young Roman Emperor — couldn't be made absurd even by that ridiculous appli-ance, and nothing could affect the unboyish wisdom in his eyes. I was standing at the window watching the sub-warden by the great box-hedge, frowningly intent on the Plato which he was carrying. His whole lean figure suggested an angry footnote. It was hardly fanciful to express it as *ut putide emendavit Adam* (his Cambridge rival). One of the Wadham owls underlined the comment with a derisory hoot. The sub-warden observed with surprise that the page was growing illegible, and concluding that this might have some connection with the descent of night, moved slowly, followed according to legend, by the owl, to-wards the gate in the archway that led to the front quad. The gate clanged and the garden was quiet. The trees settled with a sigh into their nocturnal gravity. The cedar was hardly green, the copper-beech laid aside its dyes. The owls had completed the evening ritual.

I felt a touch on my shoulder. Drum, as he very rarely did, had laid his hand there, and we stood together looking out. Flecker would have been able to express that, he said, Humbert. Flecker! I said with a snort that was more than half a sigh. You fool, he said, you poor dear fool. What can a metaphysician do? He can die, I said a little sullenly, quoting the Nietzsche aphorism. We can all do that, he said. He took down the Anthology that Morrison had extravagantly bought, and read the Erinna epitaph, of which the last two lines are:

$$\hat{\eta} \; \dot{\rho}\alpha \; \tau\acute{o}\delta' \; \breve{\epsilon}\mu\phi\rho\omega\nu$$
$$\epsilon\hat{\iota}\pi' \; \dot{\epsilon}\tau\acute{\upsilon}\mu\omega\varsigma \; \dot{\alpha} \; \pi\alpha\hat{\iota}\varsigma. \; \text{``}B\alpha\sigma\kappa\alpha\nu o\varsigma \; \breve{\epsilon}\sigma\sigma', \; \text{'}A\ddot{\iota}\delta\alpha.\text{''}$$

Poets die too, he said, but they live first. Flecker's not a poet, I answered. And you wouldn't be, if you could. No, I said stoutly. Poor dear fool, he said again. And then Gilliat came in.